Confessions of Daddy's Girl

Stories of Love, Faith, and Relationships

Sharon Patterson

Published by Beulah Publishing
Editing by ChristianEditingServices.com
Cover design by Brilliance Design and photo by iStock

Library of Congress Control Number: 2017950062
International Standard Book Number: 978-0-692-91964-4

Acknowledgments

My labor of love, writing *Confessions*, was assigned to me in 2005. Five years later I began writing my thoughts on paper. Within two years I had a manuscript of many books, from which God led me to focus on one chapter: fatherhood.

God blessed me with an awesome focus group who allowed me to keep it real: Felicia, Malika, Angie, Tanya, London, Debra, Charnita, Shauntia, Sonsyrea, Cheryl, John, Brandon, and many others who shared their daddy, love, and faith stories with me. The journey seemed to be long, but thanks to my sister circle encouraging me and sharing tidbits of their stories as daughters and as mothers raising princesses, the work was completed: Sonya, Karen, Sylvia, Janice, Morene, Fatima, Carmen S., Yvette, Kue, and many others. A special shout-out to Sisters of Thunder and Titus 2 Ministries. Many warm thanks to my "sheroes," two in particular: Yvonne Jones and Mrs. Reiss. Your courageous stories inspired me.

Special Thanks

Many years ago, my pastor prophesied that I would write many books. I held on to those powerful words. Thank you, Apostle Dr. Carmen Y. Lattimore, for seeing the best in me and supporting me through my growth. Yvonne R., you were there in the beginning; your creative direction led me through many pages. Rosemary C., you told me the truth, even when I didn't want to hear it. Janice M., you told me to possess my blessing. Sylvie E., your die-hard friendship is a blessing. Alicia A., you simply believed in me! Jen Miller, my editor, you summed up this journey as "a beautiful work, clearly woven by a perfect Father through the imperfect hands of two like-hearted daughters."

Mom, you supported me through my daddy issues without judgment. I love you!

Very Special Thanks

Abba Daddy, my personal journey through the process to reconciliation was amazing. Your patience allowed me to give voice to many, including three important men I love: my stepdad, Daniel M. Cassel, and my dad, James H. Nathan (both of whom I miss); and my husband, Lawrence—you have been so patient in allowing me the time and space to write. Your insightful wisdom gave me a different perspective toward completing this book. Thank you, my love, my friend, my Boaz.

Finally, this book is dedicated to all the young women I had the privilege to mentor. You opened up to me and shared a part of you. Each of you is remarkable!

CONTENTS

INTRODUCTION

As we nibbled on our pizza, my mentees conversed on subjects like same-sex relationships, pornography, faith challenges, finding purpose, and more. These curious high school girls were seeking to find their place in life, and social media was exposing them to adult situations, causing the teens to mature faster than they could understand. One of the girls said to me, "You're my best adult friend ever!" I laughed with amazement that I had made her A-list of friends. As we sipped our waters, we got back to the main subject of the day: boys.

While mentoring, I've met many young women who were raised primarily by their moms or other female figures. Most were desperate for answers concerning their relationship problems. They were ages fifteen, eighteen, twenty-five . . . each trying to navigate through a system of skewed values that set them up to fail. I've stood in the gap for many young women through their growing pains. Whether they needed healing, answers, or understanding, I took their problems to God in prayer and discussed with my sister circle how we might best save our baby sisters. I came to this conclusion: The root of most relationship issues stems from seeds of rebellion, lack of purpose, and dishonoring one's dad; and those seeds are planted when a dad is emotionally absent.

A dad's lack of investment in his daughter may encourage and even push her into many unsafe places and situations. Entering into unsafe circumstances, like making bad choices in relationships, stems from deeper emotional issues that make women vulnerable, exhausted, tired, and thirsty.

Jesus understood where and how women suffer emotionally. He cared enough to visit the Samaritan woman He met at the well. Their one-on-one conversation radically changed her life forever. She had known about faith, but through her lifestyle choices she was denying the power of God to live that faith to the fullest. Jesus told her to go call her husband and come back. When she replied truthfully, "I have no husband," Jesus acknowledged her confession with further truth: "You have had five husbands, and the man you now have is not your husband" (John 4:17–18 NIV).

She avoided the truth by discussing controversial religious topics of the day, clearly indicating she wasn't ready to deal with the deeper issues of her past or present. But Jesus knew the real needs of her heart. He knew she longed for a love she'd never had, likely due to an emotionally absent dad. Jesus revealed the solution she had been searching for in her past marriages and with her present live-in boyfriend: Jesus was the "living water" that would satisfy her deepest thirst for love (John 4:10 NIV). He was her Redeemer, her Maker, and the Lover of her soul. He had taken a detour to find her—a woman who wanted to be made whole, who needed to be validated, affirmed, and loved unconditionally rather than judged for her life choices. She dropped everything to tell others about Jesus's liberating power that had changed her perspective on love, faith, and relationships.

I wrote *Confessions of Daddy's Girl* for the same reasons: to tell all my baby sisters in Christ, their mothers, and all the women who give them emotional and spiritual support about the liberating power of Jesus. Sharing the testimonies of several women, including my own, demonstrates how faith in Jesus Christ helped us work through our daddy issues and led us to embrace healthy, whole, and trusting relationships.

Many of my mentees didn't know about their total benefit package—*The Blessing*—accessible the moment they accepted Jesus as Savior. Through the priceless gift of salvation, we are no longer daddy-less daughters without an inheritance; instead, we are daughters adopted by God the Father and crowned as princesses of His abundant Kingdom. Therefore, we have full access to the promises of God: for deliverance, provision, healing, fulfilled purpose, eternal life, fruitful relationships, and praise-worthy legacies, to name only a few.

Throughout *Confessions of Daddy's Girl* we will look closely at the confessions of the young women I've mentored, the circumstances that derailed them, and the steps they took to gain freedom. And we'll take a close look at fully possessing *The Blessing* from the King of kings.

I don't have all the answers toward healing our earthly daddy-daughter issues, but *if you desire to be loved in a pure and complete way and want the assurance that when you call on Abba Daddy* (translated *Daddy Daddy!*), *He will answer*, keep reading! Discover in these pages your own reconciliation journey, a safe place of healing.

I invite you to come, drink, and be satisfied. You are loved as Abba Daddy's girl!

Note: Some names in the following chapters have been changed to protect the identity and privacy of individuals whose stories are shared in this book. Some stories are a compilation of experiences that may sound similar to yours, but they are the stories of those who have shared directly with me. Relax and enjoy your reading.

ABBA DADDY!

For ye have not received the spirit of bondage again to fear; but ye have received the Spirit of adoption, whereby we cry, Abba, Father. (Romans 8:14 KJV)

Throughout this book I will refer to our heavenly Father as Abba Daddy and our earthly fathers as simply dad. Each time the word "Abba" (ah-b*uh*) is used in the Bible, it means "father" and carries a sense of "warm affection and filial confidence."[1]

---

[1]Entry for "Abba" in Baker's Evangelical Dictionary of Theology. Edited by Walter A. Elwell (Baker Books: Grand Rapids, 1996). All rights reserved. Used by permission. http://www.biblestudytools.com/dictionary/abba/ (29 April 2017).

part one

Daddy's Little Girl

✤

While in prayer I saw a vision of a young woman buried beneath many heavy, thick blankets. The dream revealed that too often a woman may not know the real woman inside herself. To become acquainted with the woman God created you to be, begin by removing the layers of your hurts and disappointments. Some issues are rooted in your childhood experiences, but wherever they are from, they prevent you from emerging into the beautiful, reigning princess God designed you to be. If this describes you, stop and ask yourself what you're searching for and what you're thirsty for. Only God has the capacity to touch, heal, and satisfy the deepest recesses of your soul and to cover you as a dad should.

Chapter One

Real Places:
Abba Daddy Saves

· ⁓ Sherry's Confession · ⁓

S herry was single, twenty-one, and pregnant by a married man. This was her sixth pregnancy and the first baby she wanted to keep. She feared that the effects from her five abortions could cause her to lose the baby. She was afraid and came to me for help. I asked if she had consulted anyone else about her dilemma. Sherry's mom and dad were unavailable to counsel her on options, so her aunties stepped in—and advised her to end the pregnancy. Her boyfriend not only agreed but threatened to leave her if she didn't have an abortion. This was a familiar place for Sherry, repeating the same choices that always bound her in similar situations: another pregnancy with another uncommitted man. Sherry was just like her aunties; they had each experienced the same repetitive circumstances. In other words, Sherry and her aunties were trapped in a generational cycle of poor choices but didn't realize it. Through much counseling, Sherry decided to go through with the pregnancy. After eight months of difficulty, she birthed a healthy baby boy. This is Sherry's story; now let's talk about yours.

CR ЄO

When bills are due, relationships are strained, and jobs are demanding, who has time to effectively parent our baby girls? The most common issue today is absentee parents using a variety of "pacifiers" in place of parenting—for example, enabling, not checking unhealthy behaviors, and giving gifts out of guilt instead of giving quality time. When our daughters are being challenged emotionally and morally, who has time to pray, fast, and listen to God or to our daughters?

I've witnessed young women singing in the church choir, serving on the usher board, and excelling in school but never experiencing a personal relationship with their Almighty Father. How is it possible for our daughters to be raised in Christian homes when parents have never presented the gospel message of salvation to them, never had family prayer with them, and never had home Bible studies with them? Is this your story?

Young women have shared with me their real-life family experiences: the fights between Mom and Dad, siblings competing with one another, Mom's unexpected anger when Dad leaves her to raise their children alone, or living in a non-traditional or blended family. For some, Daddy lived at home, but he was emotionally (and therefore spiritually) unavailable. For others, they never knew their dads. Was this your situation?

When I talked with young women about their daddy circumstances, some agreed it was difficult to have healthy connections with men because they had had poor relationships with their dads. Madison, a producer for a major sports network, confirmed this. Let's take a look at her confession as she evaluates how her dad's choices affected her views and relationships regarding men.

— *Madison's Confession: Eight Sisters, Six Mothers, and One Dad* —

Growing up, my eight sisters and I laughed and sang to Sister Sledge's song "We are Family." While that sounds warm and united, my reality involved explaining to people that out of eight sisters, only two of us shared the same mom, but we all shared the same dad. At times it was awkward introducing my half-siblings as my sisters and their mothers as my aunties to my childhood friends, who were as confused about my situation as I was. My sisters and I all mirrored some similarities from our shared dad: complexion, mannerisms, and his infectious laugh. One sister is only nine months apart from me. Some were conceived during my parents' marriage—never mind how my mom felt about his philandering. She and my aunties were distressed by his unfaithfulness. I seriously wondered if a man could be faithful to one woman because my dad certainly had not, in a big way. I loved my sisters and would not trade them for the world, but the truth of our real-life circumstance influenced our choices in men. Even though we each desired a faithful man as a spouse, we were each caught in a generational cycle of choosing men who behaved like our dad.

C3 &O

When parents, especially dads, make decisions to do things their own way instead of God's way, they're choosing to go against the One who desires to lead them to success, blessings, and prosperity, not only for themselves but also for their children.[1] This was the case for Sherry and Madison, who suffered from unhealthy relationships.

Take an inventory of your family tree. What proclivities, mindsets, cycles, illnesses, habits, and addictions are being repeated through your family line? What is your family's story?

What is Your Reality?

Did your mom try to shoulder the role of both mom and dad because your dad had left your family? Maybe he was home but hit your mom or you—or both of you. Perhaps he was in prison or was an alcoholic. Maybe your grandma raised you because your parents had abandoned you, or perhaps one or both of your parents were on drugs or died of AIDS. Possibly your dad touched you inappropriately, breeching his relationship with you. Or it could be that your dad passed away while you were young. There are many scenarios that create the reality of an absentee dad. Who, then, will be an advocate for your cause? Who will hear your cry and deliver you?

> I rescued the poor who cried for help, and the fatherless who had none to assist them. (Job 29:12 NIV)

A lot of daughters are crying, especially in the areas of wanting true love, marriage, and family. Zoe is one of them. She's coming to terms about her family's generational cycle of broken relationships. She sought answers by asking her mom relevant questions, and she understands that she's not alone as a daughter without a dad to be an example of husband-hood in the home. With no real solutions, Zoe continues to cry out.

⁓ *Zoe's Confession: When, Lord? When Will It Be My Turn?* ⁓

Mom and I were enjoying a sunny, warm afternoon together, laughing and conversing about things that matter. It felt right to say to her, "Mom, I've been seeking God about my purpose in life, and there are some things that don't make sense to me."

She asked, "What is it, Baby?"

I said, "I noticed that, like me, most of my cousins aren't married."

"Maybe they don't *want* to be married," she replied.

"Mom, I want to be married, and our family's lifestyle isn't normal in that regard."

She retorted, "What is *normal?*"

I explained, "It's not normal for a generation of women to be single or to be single with children. Something's wrong with this picture." Mom expressed that she didn't think anything of it one way or the other. But I knew in my heart that we were experiencing the consequences of past and present life choices. I asked her, "What behaviors are we repeating that result in divorce and baby-daddy drama?" She couldn't answer that, so I continued the conversation by stressing the importance of sharing our stories so that we would be equipped to make better life decisions in the future.

Mom admitted her part in the cycle by offering, "When you were young, I didn't talk to you about my relationships because my mother didn't talk to me about such things. But now I'm in a different place to talk."

With that invitation, I shared with her what I knew about our painful family secrets. But I felt her resistance and decided it was best to change the subject to something more pleasant.

I know I'm not alone in questioning God for answers. In fact, I encounter many attractive, spiritual, successful women who have not married. Some are arriving in their thirties, some are approaching their forties, and others are celebrating their fifties. I wonder if my married friends are truly content and if life on the other side—marriage—is truly blissful.

My girlfriend and I joke about our singleness, but we know in our hearts that we're part of a generation waiting to be seated (married) and then seeded (children). I wonder if a generational curse is affecting my family and others. Who will sympathize with us? Who will cry aloud and say that it's our God-given right to experience successful marriage, have beautiful children, and live peacefully? *Right, Momma?* I asked her silently from my heart. This was my cry.

(ॐ ৪০)

There's Hope!

Life circumstances and relational realities are as varied as the women who suffer from and survive them. But the end result for most is often the same: they're affected by a generational cycle, also known as a generational curse. Because the bloodline of a dad is the connectivity by which these curses continue, they can't be broken through self-help pursuits or through palm readers, juju practitioners, or one's own willpower. Generational curses can be broken only through the bloodline of a perfect and pure father, untainted by sin and bad choices. Only our heavenly Father fits this description. He is the Rock we can depend on to change our life courses! His deeds are perfect. Everything He does is just and fair; He is a faithful God who does no wrong. How just and upright He is![2] The *only* passageway for us to be grafted into our heavenly Father's bloodline is through His Son, Jesus Christ, the answer and solution for our sufferings.[3]

> They have defeated him by the blood of the Lamb. (Revelation 12:11)

When you apply the name and blood of Jesus Christ to any circumstance, you are applying the power of God that breaks the cycle of generational curses. Your adversary (Satan) will bow down to the blood of Jesus; therefore, you can experience healing from your most difficult family situations. You don't have to live under your old realities. Instead, you can live under the new covenant and possess *The Blessing* that brings peace of mind, great prosperity, unmerited promotion, unseen protection, and fruitful relationships.

Whatever was your growing-up experience—your family issues and circumstances, the choices you've made, and the choices your dad or mom made—the fact remains that you were born into your particular family and circumstances for a purpose. And I believe our heavenly Father is saying to you, "I placed you there to become a gift and a blessing—a light in the darkness." I assure you that God has chosen you to partake of *The Blessing*.

> The message of the cross is foolish to those who are headed for destruction! But we who are being saved know it is the very power of God. (1 Corinthians 1:18)

You have two options in how you will respond to the many benefits God is offering you: you can run away from His costly gift of salvation, or you can embrace it. Salvation is the good news that God has made provisions to restore the deepest issues of your life, to transform every bad thing into good, every ugliness into beauty, and to "give you hope and a future" (Jeremiah 29:11 NIV). *The Blessing* begins by welcoming Jesus Christ into your heart because He is the door to God's heart.[4] If you've never said a prayer of faith with commitment to God, read the following prayer in faith with me now:

> "Dear Heavenly Father, I know that I'm a sinner. And I ask for your forgiveness. I believe your son, Jesus, died for my sins and rose from the dead. I turn from my sins. I repent of my sins. I invite you to come into my heart and life. I want to trust and follow you as my Lord and Savior. In Jesus' name. Amen."[5]

If you prayed from your heart, believing, then you have entered into a new position reserved for the adopted daughters of Abba Daddy, the King of kings. Now all the generations that will flow from your bloodline can be forever changed for the glory of God. Your proactivity to choose God's way in every area of your life is the foundation on which your children and theirs will be born and will experience *The Blessing* of a loving God.

> Understand, therefore, that the Lord your God is indeed God. He is the faithful God who keeps his covenant for a thousand generations and lavishes his unfailing love on those who love him and obey his commands. (Deuteronomy 7:9)

Now come, drink, and learn what it means to be a princess fathered by the Most High God, bearing the inheritance of *The Blessing*!

---

[1]*Read Exodus 20:5.*

[2]*Read Deuteronomy 32:4.*

[3]*Read Colossians 1:19–20 and Galatians 3:13–14.*

[4]*Read John 14:6.*

[5]*"My Hope: Simply Sharing Jesus." Billy Graham Evangelistic Association. 2017. https://myhopewithbillygraham.org/program/lose-to-gain (Accessed February 24, 2017.)*

Chapter Two

Broken Promises:
Abba Daddy Hears

· ⁓ Charlotte's Confession · ⁓

Saturday noon. With my suede wedge heels, pink Capris, dippity-do curls, Jackie-O sunshades, and a grape Blow Pop in cheek, sitting crossed-legged on my front porch, I was ready—and waiting again. Four hours had passed. He'd done it again. My dad had stood me up. *Why does he make promises to me that he doesn't keep?* I had asked myself that question many times. He had agreed to pick me up at noon. I waited four hours for his phone call, and I would keep waiting for the next three days. That didn't come either. All I really wanted was to hear his voice and the way he said my nickname, "Peaches."

My dad was the first man to disappoint me, and I vowed I would never be disappointed like that again. I know it's a dichotomy, but my dad was also the image of perfection and someone I had adored and loved when I was young.

The downfall began with a painful divorce between my parents. I can't explain the inner turmoil I suffered, but I can say I thought it was my fault when my daddy stopped coming around. I perceived that he was rejecting me, and I became increasingly hungry for his attention and affection. When he didn't meet those needs, I sought to meet them in friendships with popular peers as I merged into young adulthood—into a fast lifestyle of doing things my way. After all, it was *my* life and *my* choice, and in my eyes, my choices were right.

Each time Dad stood me up, life would still continue, and I'd eventually forget his infractions. He had an influential way about him, so no matter what he did wrong (though it hurt and confused me each time), he could make another promise and hope would rise in me, and I'd believe him all over again. At some point I accepted with disappointment that my dad might not do what he promised. He had taught me by example that I could trust *no one's* word.

CR &O

When a dad has disappointed his daughter over and over, it's hard for her to trust anyone, ever. Parents may not know until later in life how a child has been impacted by their messy divorce, intense arguments, divisive favoritism, and negative words. These can push children into emotional and psychological isolation, prompting them to deal with stresses through destructive behaviors like self-injury, eating disorders, substance abuse, and promiscuity. Destructive choices are apparent to me each time I begin to delve more deeply into a relationship with young women I meet. At first I'm excited as I learn about their academic pursuits, hobbies, and passions; but then as we move deeper into the matters of their hearts, we often uncover their root struggles, which can usually be traced back to their upbringing. One critically important struggle is young women's estranged relationships with their dads.

A sorority club at a well-known university asked me to speak on teen pregnancy. I arrived to a full house of well-dressed, polished young ladies. I had prepared all my stats on infant mortality rates and the available resources for prenatal care, but as I began to talk, the discussion shifted and I asked, "How many of you have a good relationship with your dad?" Less than thirty percent raised their hands. These young ladies began to pour their hearts out to me about their daddy dilemmas—how trust had been broken by their dads. I gave them an opportunity to openly share their hearts. After the workshop many of the women confessed that they were ready to deal with the deep-rooted issues of rejection, anger, and self-hatred. On the surface, just looking at them or engaging in casual conversation, I would not have known their inner pain. It was by their courage to confess it all aloud that they took their first steps toward healing.

A Time to Be Honest

I've listened to women's confessions about growing up in families where the disappointments of broken promises and unfulfilled commitments were normal. They expressed how they longed for a close relationship with their daddies but eventually lost hope when their expectations weren't met. As little girls, they didn't shed a tear or speak a word to God, themselves, or anyone else about their resentment and unforgiveness toward their dads. They covered their wounds with emotional bandages and got busy with life. These women achieved great accomplishments, thinking their successes would hide the inadequacies they felt inside. But over time, their dysfunctional, disappointing relationships with their dads, consequently, transferred with others.

How can you be whole if you're emotionally arrested? How can you move forward with love if your heart is broken? How can you find peace if you've never acknowledged your disappointments? How can you be all Abba designed you to be if you're subconsciously viewing yourself as Daddy's wounded girl? This is a pitiful place to be.

I was once immersed in that place, wanting a real, authentic connection with my dad, but I didn't know how. It was exhausting for me to go through life always searching for the perfect someone or the perfect job, vacation, or experience, only to realize that none of these things could compensate for my desire to have a close relationship with my dad. In order for me to be real, I had to sincerely work through my unforgiveness and pride. I was going to church and loving others, but my heart was as hard as stone toward my dad. I was praying to Abba, but I couldn't pick up the phone to call my dad. I was involved in community projects, but I didn't have compassion for my dad. Abba saw my heart's desire, beyond the façade of my good works, and He answered my prayers by gently opening my eyes to these revelations about my own human nature:

> I disappointed others, I failed to follow through on commitments, and I broke promises I couldn't keep. I realized I was an imperfect daughter who was the product of an imperfect dad. Abba lovingly enlightened me to my lack of perfection, which was very humbling. But these insights gave me the courage to trust Abba and drop the charges I had held against my dad for so long. Now, when I see my earthy dad, I see through the eyes of a daughter who truly loves her dad through his imperfections; for truly Abba Daddy is our perfect Daddy.

Confession Leads to Trust

If you've ever struggled with trusting others, you're more likely to have trust issues with Abba Daddy as well. It's common to transfer distrust toward Abba Daddy because subconsciously He represents the father figure who hurtfully disappointed you. Trust requires *practice* when this natural ability has been stolen from you. And prayer—an intimate communication with God—is the starting place. Therefore, when you pray, give Abba Daddy praise and thanks, and then ask Him to listen closely to your prayers of need and your heart's desires. He will hear your confession and petitions, and He will answer you. You can trust Abba Father.

> Those who know your name trust in you, for you, O Lord,
> do not abandon those who search for you. (Psalm 9:10)

The mystical work of trust begins with confession. Just as a loving daddy-daughter relationship is built on communication, your relationship with Abba Daddy is as strong as your confessions. True relationship is being honest enough to trust Him with your hurts, disappointments, and failures. It's okay to acknowledge to Him how you feel, because there's no shame or fear in the circle of love between you and your Abba Daddy.

> Trust in the Lord with all your heart, and lean not on your
> own understanding; in all your ways acknowledge Him,
> and He will direct your paths. (Proverbs 3:5–6 MEV)

Healthy, Whole, and Trusting Relationships

Today is the day to start believing that Abba wants *you* to have healthy, whole, and trusting relationships. But godly relationships must begin with *you*! You cannot afford to waste time and energy waiting on others to make the first move to begin a godly relationship with you. In your steps of faith, Abba will provide all that you need to *THRIVE* as His princess. He will give you strength, courage, and discernment in all your relationships as you practice trusting Him and believing in true love again.

Chapter Three

Unprotected Places:
Abba Daddy Heals

─ *Laura's Confession* ─

The very establishment that was supposed to protect me failed me.

❧ ❧

> For the brokenness of the daughter of my people I am
> broken; I mourn, dismay has taken hold of me. Is there
> no balm in Gilead? Is there no physician there? Why
> then has not the health of the daughter of my people
> been restored? (Jeremiah 8:21–22 NASB)

If you've experienced any form of abuse, you know what it feels like to be unprotected and insecure. The abuse, regardless of the type or extent, was a violation to your soul that caused you deep pain. It left you with a gaping wound and bound you in a dark prison cell within yourself. No one protected you or stood up for you as a child. Perhaps you shared your experiences with someone you thought you could trust, like your mom or grandmother, but when you took that step of faith, nothing changed. Maybe you weren't believed, which crushed you all the more. Whatever your circumstances, you vowed to keep silent.

The dark, secret place that women have most admitted to is childhood sexual abuse. "It includes direct sexual contact, the adult or otherwise older person engaging indecent exposure . . . to a child with intent to gratify their own sexual desires."[1] You may not have experienced an overtly degrading sexual assault, but if you were sexually disrespected in *any* way, you were sexually violated, and that compromised your innocence, dignity, and feelings of worth.

I've sat with girls who were crying for help, confessing to me how their mothers' boyfriends targeted them, the babysitters' brothers fondled them, the gang rapes devastated them, close relatives sexually exposed and exploited them—and sharing how they were consequently living with those ugly, deep secrets.

The injustices that took place when you were young may still be weighing heavily inside you like an unsolved crime. In fact, your memory may easily be triggered by something or someone, and the feelings tied to your victimization may suddenly wash over you again in the form of flashbacks and body memories. You may be physically twenty-one, but emotionally you're still a tender five-year-old. Perhaps you're thirty-two, but in the gentleness of your feelings you're still age ten. Maybe you're past middle age, but you can instantly recall the silent tears you cried as a lonely sixteen-year-old.

Because of unresolved hurts from abusive experiences, you may feel that your experiences are too painful to talk about; you may be struggling with feelings of guilt, anger, shame, and even depression.

You may still be set on making someone—anyone—pay for what happened to you. You also may still feel victimized. This prison cell of dark emotions is real, and a lot of women are living there in secret, feeling alone and powerless. If you're living with such bondage from your childhood memories and emotions, you are *not* alone, you are not crazy, and you are not powerless.

I've ministered to countless women who were sexually violated and didn't have a dad to protect them from the abuser or to cover them through their pain. As a result, these beautiful souls were constantly searching for emotional protection, hoping that a man—any man—would provide this missing piece. There are countless incidents of sexual abuse in various forms and degrees that lead young women to gravitate toward and even pursue unprotected places. Laura's story describes one of them.

⁓ *Laura's Confession* ⁓

My story began with the withered hands and perverse eyes of predatory men who stole my opportunity to experience true love on my terms. Others were judging my relational fruit without knowing my root. They weren't interested in my story, just my struggle. They said my relationships resembled the changing seasons. My life became so bad that I didn't even breathe between breakups. I just thought I was wired that way—until Abba Daddy whispered to me, "What are you searching for? I am He!"

I needed to know God better, closer, in a new and personal way. For four years He separated me from others so that He could more fully show me His pure and unconditional love. In His presence I learned how to be solely dependent on Him for my emotional and spiritual needs rather than seeking fulfillment in temporary romances that always led me back into darkness and loneliness. Some know this separation from worldly desires as *sanctification*—a preparation process for a greater, divine purpose beyond my life plans. During this period of solitude with Jesus, I learned to hear the voice of God's Spirit living in me, and I kept a journal of the profound moments of intimate conversation we shared. I heard His spirit say to mine,"No more dependencies on unhealthy relationships; no more crutches as lame excuses." This was my *aha* moment of understanding. I realized it was time for me to stop running away from my problems and face them in a real and truthful way. And boy, did God ever bring change in me!

As I sat quietly with Him in prayer, He brought to my remembrance life incidents that still felt very uncomfortable to me—the sexual violations I'd experienced as a child when I was fondled and touched inappropriately by various men. Those memories had been repressed in me because as a young child I didn't have the cognitive ability to process such violations. The memories were of men who had been trusted to look after me: my babysitter's son, my grandmother's male friend, and an older cousin. I don't know how I ended up in each of their laps, but that's where my memories took me every single time. At that young age I thought their laps were where I was supposed to be; no one had taught me otherwise. Something about their touches infused in me the belief that such intimate activity is a way to gain male attention and acceptance. But in my quietness with God, He set me free by showing me these truths: those touches were by perverted men with withered hands, and their vulgar touches were sin against me physically, emotionally, mentally, and spiritually. They were also sins against my holy heavenly Father. The poison of their touches had transferred death to my spirit, killed my innocence, and stolen my virtue and dignity and my ability to recognize and set boundaries. Their lustful hands had transferred the black spirit of lust to me, blinding me from seeing my true worth, tying me up, and rewiring me in confusion, distrust, and an insatiable need for true love—pure love. That lust lured me to live out my teenage years in the only way I knew how to feel loved: promiscuity.

I subconsciously sought out similar experiences of fake love from fake father figures, not realizing how I was perpetuating the harm within me. Instead of finding healthy relationships, I attracted dogs and wolves who violated me further and reinforced what I had come to believe about myself: I'm nothing; I'm an object; I'm worthless; I have no value and no purpose other than to be the fleshly food for predators of this world.

The ravenous desert land of my spirit drove me further into sin, farther into dry and thirsty places as I searched desperately for my true Protector and the true Lover of my soul. Finally finding Jesus was my season to be made whole as I dwelled in His quiet, gentle, healing presence. Abba created for me a warm and protective internal home with Him, where I began to see truth clearly and embrace it: a safe home in which to be vulnerable to admit to myself and to Him that I had been sexually violated in monstrous ways; a safe home to unleash my anger, to mourn all that had been stolen from me, to break my silence, and to gain the courage to seek help from others.

The little girl inside me still cried with questions: *Where was my daddy? Where was my mommy? Where was God? Where was my protector? Where was love?* Those questions were okay for me to ask, because in the shelter of Abba's wings I learned that love—true, pure, and whole love—was there in Him and dwelling within me. The evidence is in the fact that I'm not only still living but thriving! And I have an important, critical story to tell others: Abba Daddy can heal the deepest hurts.

☙ ❧

There is healing for Abba's daughters.
He is the great physician who restores!

Abba is the Father who heals bitter situations. He assures that healing is one of the blessings you can claim when you place your faith in Jesus Christ.

> Let all that I am praise the Lord; may I never forget the good things he does for me. He forgives all my sins and heals all my diseases. (Psalm 103:2–3)

As His adopted daughter, you possess His pure bloodline and have His supernatural power at work in your daily life. Therefore, His desire is for you to be *whole* and *free* from emotional, mental, and spiritual bondage. He has a unique purpose for your new life in Him.

> Call to me and I will answer you and tell you great and unsearchable things you do not know. (Jeremiah 33:3 NIV)

These "unsearchable things" include the hidden layers within you that have been buried beneath a lot of generational pain, as perhaps they buried your grandmother, your mother, and even your daughter within their sexual abuse experiences. Take a moment to get alone with your Abba Father and become vulnerable. Be still, get quiet, and let Him minister to you. When

He touches the spots that hurt, cry out to Him! Don't be afraid to call on your Heavenly Father. He will hear your cry and respond. Cry until tears flow from your eyes; cry until you can't cry anymore. In the stillness of the moment, He will wipe away your tears, touch you with His peace and healing, and cover your most vulnerable places! Now *that* is the true, authentic, and perfect LOVE of a Father. *That* is where true restoration to *new life* begins.

---

[1] *Wikipedia contributors, "Sexual abuse," Wikipedia, The Free Encyclopedia, https://en.wikipedia.org/w/index.php?title=Sexual_abuse&oldid=771122571 (Accessed February 24, 2017.)*

part two

The Journey to Perfect Love

A llison shared her most intimate secrets with me. She confessed that she left Machai, whom she had met on social media, for Kevin, her grade school sweetheart. She had a friend with special benefits named Logan, whom she used in order to get back at Kevin because Kevin had posted a picture of himself with her "bestie"; then she hooked up with Molly, her latest love interest. I suspected that relationship would last for only a season.

Even though Allison's faith had taught her one set of values, her choices in relationships spoke volumes to what she really believed about herself. She didn't think well of herself because she believed the lie that she was not worthy of perfect love. She was famished for acceptance and fearful of being alone. Because Allison allowed her fears to dominate her choices, her lifestyle of expiring relationships had become her norm. She came to me for counsel.

I realized we had had similar struggles with the fear of loneliness. As she was speaking I had a flashback of my life: I was young, discovering myself, and searching for love, not realizing that perfect love had been there all along. I simply had not embraced it. This was my opportunity to share my story with her. "Do you have a big sister?" I asked. She responded no. So I became her sister for those fleeting but precious thirty minutes.

"There are some things you must know about perfect love as you grow into womanhood," I began. "Perfect love is not a desperate feeling of anxiousness. You may not realize you're making desperate decisions until you've had four or five boyfriends. That's a lot of boyfriends and many disappointments too! Perfect love is to embrace Abba Daddy—who is *pure love*—as your maker, husband, and redeemer.[1] He will satisfy you and make you complete, because every good thing you desire comes from Him through *The Blessing*."[2]

Covenant of Faithfulness: My Own Confession

The Blessing opened the door to my design career. Design was my passion and where my true gift was rooted. I didn't have to sift through various activities to figure that out; I knew at a young age what I wanted to do. I spent time cultivating my gift, and Abba Daddy gave me success. His unique plan for me to fulfill His good purpose was to work in the entertainment and broadcast industries. I found these fields very rewarding, not only because He had planted this desire and gift in me but also because He had empowered me to use these to produce successful promotions and advertisements for companies. He had anointed me with creativity and favor that resulted in winning a number of prestigious awards. These immense highlights in my career were a personal blessing from Abba Daddy as a result of my choice to follow Him.

At this point you may be wondering what spiritual purpose God could possibly have had for me working successfully in such a secular, Christian-controversial industry. Abba Daddy used that environment to grow me spiritually. There were times when my loyalty to Him was shaken by various temptations that tested the foundation of my faith. I learned a great deal about Abba's perfect love, and He would later use that knowledge for my good in ministry to other women. One key lesson was the battle between my own desires and His desires for me. My true confession is that I went astray during the most career-fruitful time in my life, and I experienced the fact that His faithfulness to me and His perfect love for me were solid.

The Entertainment Bubble

Early in my career I befriended young women like myself who were looking for opportunities. We were fresh, invisible, and hungry to find ourselves, and we found a lot of options. We were living life on the edge, making money, and discovering life through the glitter and fake-gold lenses of the world—lenses tinted with images of en vogue dresses, hourglass figures, long weaves, and short-lived boyfriends. We were mesmerized by the music business and all that came with it: record company reps, makeup artists, stylists, and on-air personalities. We witnessed the jet-set lifestyle of recording artists and had access to backstage productions and VIP parties. Some of us were satisfied to just live on the peripheral of the action, but others wanted more, a piece of the dream, and for some girls that meant by any means necessary. They descended into the belly of the entertainment beast, which required them to make an exchange with their flesh. That was the sacrifice to be up close and personal with well-known athletes, celebrities, and super stars. They gave little thought to catching a plane to a party in New York, Los Angeles, or Atlanta; it was part of the sacrifice to live the glam life. When a well-known record producer from the Mecca visited the TV station, the "it girls" were dressed very seductively to stand out, to be seen and accepted—like the video girls who played star roles for just a minute.

As we eventually found out, the entertainment bubble is make-believe, created for the screens and never for cultivating real or permanent relationships. Just like the storyline in a movie, the entertainment beast sold us the perfect dream, the flawless image, and the brand look. We also felt that we didn't have to downgrade to find a boo-mate. Nor did we feel the need to call home to check in with our daddies for the wisdom we so desperately needed. Instead, we played the daddy-less daughters, a generation of well-educated young women looking to be affirmed by eye-candy men with A-list statuses.

Rebellion eventually took its toll on our souls. Our dreams faded too soon as we played in the entertainment bubble and fed that beast with our flesh. As we approached our mid-thirties, the fast lifestyle left us feeling low, used, and alone.

Getting Back Home

One day Abba opened my eyes again, and I saw clearly that I had strayed and needed to get back to His perfect love. I realized that He is not cool with sin. This realization led me to repent and to rely on His everlasting grace and mercy as I sought to find new hope and purpose for my life. I confess that it's difficult to trust Abba Daddy when self-centered desires compete with His perfect love and plan. My desire to live life my way had been the roadblock preventing me from fulfilling my God-given purpose. When the world was telling me to go this way or that, it took drawing on the power of the Holy Spirit to hear God's voice within me instead. It took that same power for me to "walk by faith, not by sight" (2 Corinthians 5:7 ESV).

I had at last come to my senses, passionately seeking God with *all* my heart. I experienced a love that drew me closer to Him—the perfect love of the perfect Father drawing His vulnerable daughter into His arms and whispering, "I've got this, my princess. I'll lead you." His love for me superseded *all* the negativity that had shaped my thoughts, decisions, and actions. I was becoming what the apostle Paul said I could become: "If anyone is in Christ, the new creation has come: The old has gone, the new is here!" (2 Corinthians 5:17) Paul was speaking about those who seek Christ with their whole hearts; the old self is gone, and the new self has come! I was learning to see myself, dress myself, and train myself as the princess I had become through my adoption by the King of kings!

> God decided in advance to adopt us into his own family by bringing us to himself through Jesus Christ. This is what he wanted to do, and it gave him great pleasure. (Ephesians 1:5)

My Journey to Perfect Love

My journey to find perfect love began with asking God many questions about my life. These questions were a prayer journey that led me back to church. On one occasion I surveyed the congregants and saw several young women sitting in the back. I wondered if they were struggling, as I was, to make sense of God, the Bible, and church and how these three important factors fit into our purpose to have healthy relationships and find perfect love. At times I was divided in my heart about the spiritual principles taught through these avenues. How do I apply them to make right decisions? Truthfully I knew what was morally right, yet I made decisions based on my own self-interests. As a result, I suffered from those poor choices, not fully realizing that my actions were taking me farther from the fulfillment I was seeking. I had yet to learn to be obedient to the Word of God so that He would fulfill His abundant promises to me. Along my journey to find perfect love, I discovered that Jesus too had learned obedience to God through the things He suffered.[3]

During my journey I recognized that Sunday services were not enough spiritual and emotional food for the greater needs I had within. Like many people, it seemed, I had no spiritual depth or accountability from Monday through Saturday, and I considered that the young women sitting in the back of the church likely lacked the same. Many young people appeared to think as I did: we're much wiser than our predecessors—our mothers, aunties, and grandmothers—in making decisions about our lives. Only later would the stories of older and wiser women shed light on the roadblocks that were keeping us from fulfilling our destinies: to be mature, beautiful princesses of God, to live in His perfect love, and to attract the same likeness in others. We were each lacking in ourselves the foundation for healthy relationships: the perfect love of Abba as defined in 1 Corinthians 13:4–7:

> Love is patient. Love is kind. It does not want what belongs to others. It does not brag. It is not proud. It does not dishonor other people. It does not look out for its own interests. It does not easily become angry. It does not keep track of other people's wrongs. Love is not happy with evil. But it is full of joy when the truth is spoken. It always protects. It always trusts. It always hopes. It never gives up. (NIRV)

Getting to a place called *perfect love* is a process, a journey, a walk, an unfolding. It's a willingness to be vulnerable enough to admit to yourself and God the need to change and to submit to change. Admitting to Abba Daddy that change is necessary—whether in regard to love relationships, parent relationships, career, school, or church relationships—He'll divinely lead you in the direction you should go. This is the work of the Holy Spirit.

> Whether you turn to the right or to the left, your ears will
> hear a voice behind you, saying, "This is the way; walk
> in it." (Isaiah 30:21 NIV)

As I walked with Christ, I came to understand that a personal relationship with Abba Daddy is a step-by-step journey of conversation: seeking, asking, and knocking, as Matthew 7:7 encourages, and learning to recognize His voice in me. It's also a journey of faith as I try new experiences to learn which ones are in line with Abba Daddy's divine plan for my life and which ones are not.

When I began to walk by faith with Christ, putting my selfish desires aside to serve others with His perfect love, I discovered I had a passion for helping young women succeed in their own faith walks. My life purpose grew clearer to me when I chose to participate as one of the leaders of Sisters of Thunder, a young adult women's ministry. The ministry involved about seven women in their twenties meeting weekly to encourage each other in their faith walks. They were diverse in ethnicity, culture, and education, but all shared some common goals. Foremost was their thirst for God. They knew that their respective purposes were rooted in serving Him.

Also, most of them were tired of the dead-end results of their efforts to figure out their relationship issues. Those adverse results had left each of them feeling empty and subsequently led them to embrace the Bible as the absolute truth, believing in the full manifestation of *The Blessing* for marriage and children.[4] Each young woman made the personal choice to stand rooted in the Word of God and Jesus Christ, the Rock that is unmoving and unchanging.

> Truly he is my rock and my salvation; he is my fortress,
> I will never be shaken. (Psalm 62:2 NIV)

The young women began to make choices from God's kingdom principles rather than their own self-centered desires. Choosing to live according to God's Word led each to discover her individual missions beyond the desire to get married. Each had a unique, divine purpose that grew clearer as we continued to faithfully meet and pray together.

Meeting regularly to mentor these young women was the connection and participation I needed to deepen my own relationship with Christ and to hear Him more clearly say, "This is the way; walk in it." It was during that time of mentoring others that I discovered that the most beautiful characteristics He wanted me to wear were the fruit of His Spirit:

> Love, joy, peace, forbearance, kindness, goodness, faithfulness, gentleness and self-control. (Galatians 5:22–23 NIV)

I realized that wearing the garment of His righteousness and glory is evidence that I am Abba Daddy's daughter—His princess. My life became a sweet-smelling fragrance that attracted healthy relationships with others. I came to understand that practicing to be like Jesus was what the apostle Paul was speaking about when he said, "Continue to work out your salvation . . . for it is God who works in you to will and to act in order to fulfill his good purpose" (Philippians 2:12–13 NIV).

Finding Purpose

After several years of freelancing in the media business, it was time for me to transition into new territories, because Abba Daddy had an assignment for me that was dear to His heart. He called me to help rescue women and their unborn babies who visited our local pregnancy center. This was part of His unique plan for my life, and I did it unapologetically! I became a support to young women in crisis situations such as unplanned pregnancies, disparaging relationships, ill reproductive health, and faith challenges. Some were members of local churches, but when they had a crisis they sought solutions at the pregnancy center. The lessons I had learned while working in the media industry were applicable in my ministry at the center. God had placed me there to open my eyes to a community of women who desperately needed Him. At the same time, He was opening my eyes to reconcile with Him the unhealthy choices I had made in my twenties. I learned more about Abba Daddy's plan for healthy living and the obstacles that derail His daughters from their divine destinies. God's people are being destroyed because they don't know Him in the *fullness* of His might.[5]

I continued to seek God, and He opened the door for me to work in the legislative sector. There I was asked to participate in community outreach initiatives. This work gave me further insight into the complex lives of young women and their families. I was moving in my purpose and calling when I encountered people outside my culture and community. I met parents who built protective layers of mentors around their daughters' lives. And I also discovered there are some parents who are not equipped with the necessary resources to help their daughters achieve *success* academically, spiritually, emotionally, and relationally. By sharing my story with these young women, I was embracing my purpose as their sisters' keeper. There was no judgment, only the unconditional love of a big sister. I wanted to let these younger sisters know that the perfect love they were searching for is found only in a personal relationship with Abba Daddy, their Creator. I shared with them that if they placed their faith in Jesus, they would have all the rights to *The Blessing* of the Lord, which is everything they need to reach the dreams and goals God placed in their hearts and be truly successful in life.

> The blessing of the Lord makes a person rich, and he adds no sorrow with it. (Proverbs 10:22)

୧ ୨

In the following three chapters you will read how young women found strength in Abba Daddy to make different choices: to forgive, to be celibate, to put their pasts behind them, to wait on the Lord, to discover their purposes, and to embrace Abba Daddy as their *perfect love*.

---

[1] *Isaiah 54:5.*

[2] *Read Deuteronomy 8:18.*

[3] *Read Hebrew 5:8.*

[4] *Read Deuteronomy 7:13.*

[5] *Read Hosea 4:6.*

Chapter Four

Trapped Places:
Abba Daddy Frees

⌐ Emerald's Confession: Love Led Me Back Home ⌐

At 4:00 a.m. I woke up inside a drug house. I'm not sure what drug I used the night before, but I had passed out around 10:00 p.m. The bath, kitchen, and living room were occupied by people doing their drugs of choice. I searched for my friend Ava and found her slumped at the kitchen table, passed out. Hanging out with her had taught me that I'd never know where I would end up. Ava was popular. She represented everything I was told about bad girls, but I never thought my friendship with her would be the catalyst to my addiction.

I smoked a little marijuana here and popped a little pill there, but alcohol became my drug of choice. It helped to medicate the stresses of life. My addiction fooled me into thinking I was living my life as if it were golden. In truth, my addiction was bondage, and I suffered the consequences—big time. I was out of control when my addiction led me to get fired from my job and eventually expelled from a well-known, prestigious music conservatorium. I lost my scholarship I had worked so hard to get. My addiction led me to make choices that contradicted my faith and conscience, and I kept those behaviors on the down-low from my parents.

I took advantage of my dad and mom, manipulating them in any way that would benefit me, and I spoke harshly to them. My behaviors fueled intense arguments between us and later separated us. But the loss and disconnection from my parents didn't stop me from continuing to drink excessively and live a rebellious lifestyle. The pain of living up to others' expectations made me rebel all the more. I could not figure out where I was in life or what I had become, and I had no prospect of where I was going. Alcohol was what I needed to numb the pain and get through each day, but what I truly needed was a way out from my addictions.

As a preacher's daughter I knew better, but I was tired of living under my dad's rules and my family's hounding hopes for me. My dad's busy schedule meant less time for me. Compared to his higher calling, I felt less important. And let's not even talk about church folks. They ignited in me a fire to go far left from what I had been taught. So when my parents sent me off to school when I was eighteen, I was a naïve virgin who set out to defy everything I was raised to believe. By my twenty-first birthday I was jobless, homeless, and school-less.

On a rainy Sunday evening, buried in my depression, I called my dad. Before I had even uttered the question, he said, "Come home, daughter! Come home!"

I'm not going to say it was easy being back home, but I knew that somewhere in the midst of all my heartache, I was on the edge of being reborn and free! At first, returning home was like picking up where I had left off. It seemed as if nothing had changed in my family's views or expectations of me; consequently, I was faced with all those old feelings I had buried in my drugs. All those feelings reignited the conflicts in me that I had battled while previously living at home. I just didn't know how to communicate my feelings to my parents. I don't believe I felt vulnerable enough to trust my dad with my true thoughts and emotions. All I heard from him was "Clean your room, wash the dishes, vacuum the floor, find a job, and don't forget your curfew time." Rules! Rules! Rules! My attitude was familiar: I ain't submitting to nobody's rules, and don't ask me about church either, because right now I'm mad at God!

One Wednesday evening I decided to attend Bible study. Sitting in the back row, I began to cry. I felt broken. I wanted out of my addictions: alcohol, cigarettes, tattoos, and outbursts of anger. No more covering up the pain. At home that night I prayed sincerely to God: *I don't want to be this way anymore; I want to be free!*

During the next Sunday's service, the gospel song moved me from my pew to the altar. I didn't care that I was standing there alone; I just wanted my freedom, and I wanted it right then. The church mothers prayed with me as if I were their daughter. I heard their strong cries for deliverance, and I cried out too with all of my mind, my heart, and my strength. I coughed and sighed, releasing all the negativity in my heart. This spiritual experience was so powerful that it knocked me to my knees. When I stood up, I felt lighter; everything around me was quiet and brighter. I immediately embraced my dad and began to sob on his shoulder. I asked him to forgive me for all the pain I had caused him. He said, "I forgave you long ago, daughter. Please forgive *me*. I love you." His expression of love was what I needed to hear. I needed the unconditional love of a daddy who had never given up on his daughter.

Forgiving myself was not an easy process, but I thank God that He led me back to a safe place: home. Being home allowed me to deal with my hurt by reconnecting me to the source: my dad. Since that day of prayer and deliverance, I have miraculously lost my appetite for alcohol. I can't even stand the smell of it! That is the power of Abba Daddy.

It's been five years, and I haven't had a drink. Abba Daddy restored me to a place of peace and stability. I'm a youth leader, I'm back in school, I'm playing my violin again, and I'm sharing my story of how love brought me back home and how the power of forgiveness not only set me free but also healed my relationship with my dad.

03 80

I met up with Emerald for lunch during the holidays. She was sober and preparing for a major concert. She had found a circle of optimistic, drug-free friends, and she was engaged to a nice young man who performed with her in the orchestra. It was refreshing to listen to all the wonderful news about Emerald's born again new life. She had such a peace about her. I asked her how her relationship with her dad was developing. She said, "I wish every person knew that forgiveness is the key to healing. It affects every nuance of our being and the way we love others. The healing and freedom of forgiveness spill into every relationship. If we hate (or dislike) our dads, it's likely we don't get along well in other key relationships. Unforgiveness and not letting go of past issues are like fertilizing the field of bitterness. That poisonous diet will cause all types of emotional and physical ailments."

She also shared about having unconditional love for her dad and how this perfect love was helping their communication. She said,

"When I experience my dad's inconsistencies, I don't criticize him like I used to, because now I understand the power of forgiveness. We have daddy-daughter dates that give us opportunities to share what's on our hearts. Loving him and praying for him is a prescription that has helped me work through my judgment of him and my mom."

> Listen to your father, who gave you life, and don't despise your mother when she is old. (Proverbs 23:22)

Can We Talk?

How many of you were raised in church, found faith in God, but then something derailed you along the way? You began to question your faith. Maybe you wanted independence or were disenchanted by what you witnessed around you. Or you became curious about a lifestyle you were told not to emulate, and you may have resisted the parental guidance that seemed too old-fashioned. Now you may be saying, "I'm not religious, but I'm spiritual." You may be questioning the teachings of the Bible and open to accepting things that are controversial to the biblical teaching you were raised under.

Going Astray

> For the world offers only a craving for physical pleasure, a craving for everything we see, and pride in our achievements and possessions. These are not from the Father, but are from this world. (1 John 2:16)

When young women go astray, Babylon—the world system that seeks to exist without God—is waiting for them.[1] Babylon uses you when you're young and strong and spits you out when you're old and weak. How? Babylon's counterfeit system lures you with material gratification that's temporary: fame, fortune, fashion, fine cuisine, big houses, and expensive cars—the lifestyle of the rich and famous. Babylon preaches rebellion through worldly music and what *millennials* call "hype" and "lit beats." She falsely promises a cure to satisfy your core desires. If you've ever partaken of her delicacies, you know what's like to lose your soul. One day you have the personality of a movie star, and the next day you're looking like a rap star; today you're with a girl and tomorrow a guy; one season you're a Muslim and the next you're a Christian. I call this the *lost identity stage*—not realizing that what you're actually seeking is *the image* of your Creator.

When your faith is neither anchored in Jesus nor rooted in the Word of God, you'll find yourself searching for your identity—the inner part of you that makes you special and unique. Your identity cannot be found by imitating what you read in magazines, see on social media, or hear from the music you listen to. These sleek and sparkling media tools of Babylon will only give you false affirmation that will root you in materialism, drown you in insecurity, and control your mind with beta-kitten sexuality. False self-images are contradictory to the woman of substance and integrity Abba Daddy created you to be. When the lights and cameras are off, when the actresses go home, when the entertainers no longer have the mic, the souls of Babylon are still crying out for perfect love, true intimacy, and enduring security. This is why He admonishes His princesses to "come out from among unbelievers, and separate yourselves from them, says the Lord. Don't touch their filthy things, and I will welcome you" (2 Corinthians 6:17). And He promises, "I will be your God throughout your lifetime—

until your hair is white with age. I made you, and I will care for you. I will carry you along and save you" (Isaiah 46:4).

If you want to have a clear pathway to *The Blessing* that frees you from trapped places and prospers every aspect of your life, then get to know who God created you to be. He knows the plans for your life, a pathway to a celebratory end.

Rebellion Steals *The Blessing*

> He redeemed us in order that the blessing given to Abraham might come to the Gentiles through Christ Jesus, so that by faith we might receive the promise of the Spirit. (Galatians 3:14 NIV)

The adversary, the thief of *The Blessing*, will use offenses to steal your promises. Your brokenheartedness over those offenses may have caused a rift between you and your dad, between you and Abba Daddy, between you and your baby daddy, or between you and the church. When you become offended and don't work through the issues, eventually you will rebel.

> Rebellion is as sinful as witchcraft, and stubbornness as bad as worshiping idols. (Samuel 15:23)

Rebellion causes your hurt feelings to continue to haunt you, and eventually you may find yourself acting out. When conflict comes, take a moment to examine yourself and ask, "Am I possessing *The Blessing* or running away from *The Blessing*?"

To possess *The Blessing* is to have faith in God no matter what! You must exercise your faith by forgiving others and yourself and showing love after disappointing situations. You must see Abba Daddy and yourself as bigger than your problems, stand your ground by proclaiming the promises of God over your situations, and lay hold of your spiritual inheritance—this is reigning as a princess of God. You must maintain a personal prayer time, attend Bible study, consecrate yourself, and embrace your God-ordained purpose by saying yes to everything He asks of you—no compromises or exceptions.

To run away from *The Blessing* is to allow rejection, resentment, and other self-centered, self-destructive behaviors to push you over the edge, once again leading a lifestyle of wearing provocative clothing, engaging in sexting, bullying, cutting, drugging, groping, rebelling, tattooing, clubbing, chanting, lying, stealing, and even palm reading. To run from *The Blessing* is to forget that all your prosperity and successes are found in Abba Daddy through a personal relationship with Jesus Christ. He will keep you on the right and safe path.[2]

When you're in the dark place of rebellion, nobody can tell you anything because everything said to you falls on your deaf ears, especially wisdom from your dad, your mom, and your heavenly Father.

> "Honor your father and mother." This is the first commandment with a promise: If you honor your father and mother, "things will go well for you, and you will have a long life on the earth." (Ephesians 6:2–3)

To dishonor your dad is to lower his ordained position as your earthly father, which is to curse your root, your DNA, the core from which you were created, and the seed of the promise that offers you success and a long life. Abba Daddy didn't say to honor your mother and father *if* they are the best parents. Regardless of their parenting skills, God commanded you to honor (respect) your parents, because He placed them as your earthly guardians to teach, guide, and protect you. They are, in large, your connectivity to *The Blessing* that can flow freely in and through your life.

God Rewards Obedience

God rewards your obedience in honoring your appointed guardians—whether they're your biological, foster, or adoptive parents or other parental authorities. Honoring them applies to you because God placed them in authority over you as a child. Your reward for obeying His command is found in Ephesians 6:3: "So that it may go well with you and that you may enjoy long life on the earth." Here's a good example: My girlfriend gave herself a big birthday party to celebrate her fifty years of life. She paid for the party and invited her guests, including her dad. When he asked the birthday girl to do something for him, she responded, "Yes, sir!" I chuckled, because her attitude was such a refreshing show of respect that one doesn't often hear anymore.

---

[1] *Read Revelation 18:1–13.*

[2] *Read Deuteronomy 11:16.*

Chapter Five

Unsafe Places:
Abba Daddy Affirms

Mia, my thirty-something millennial friend, shared with me how she struggles with believing God's promises whenever she's faced with overwhelming challenges. When obstacles seemed too big, she'd confess excuse scenarios: "I can't because" and "What if . . . ?" Whenever she faced relationship challenges, she'd have internal dialogues like "Will he still like me if I say no? Will he love me more if I give in?" and defeating statements like "He may reject me and find someone else."

After years of weight loss challenges, Mia had become very insecure about her size and image. All her internal insecurities drove her to many yo-yo dieting plans that failed. So when Marcus Holliday took an interest in her, their love grew—and so did her self-esteem. Finally someone loved all of her, and she felt solid, secure, and beautiful. No more wondering or doubting her beauty; she was off the dating market and enjoying her relationship. When Mr. Holliday proposed, it was "like heaven," she said. It was her season, her turn to plan for her long-awaited big day: the white dress, the bridesmaid selections, the invitation mailings. All her dreams were now in one basket.

Then one day something went south with their love. Straight out of left field, her fiancé unexpectedly called off their engagement. Shocked, she asked, begged, and sought answers regarding his indifference, and each time he provided the same answers: "It's not you; it's me." Six months later she discovered he had married another woman. The shock and embarrassment shredded her self-esteem. She just couldn't shake the breakup, loss, and disappointment. She began to question herself: *Am I not good enough? Is it my weight? Was it the way I loved?*

No one knew the depth of her despair, because she was good at putting up a front, keeping up appearances by shrouding her image as the well-liked friend, sister, and daughter with great aspirations to become a recording artist. She had sung background on some nationally-known neo soul soundtracks. Her ambition seemed promising; because a music producer from New York was courting her for a record deal. Even though she knew how to be diverse with her personality and could sing like a wonder, it was difficult for her to work through all her conflicting insecurities.

Mia struggled with doubt and unbelief, which stemmed from fear. I shared with her that when adverse situations arise, you should remember Abba Daddy's character instead of dwelling on what you see, hear, and feel. I asked her, "Has Abba Daddy ever failed you?"

"No!" she emphatically replied.

"Has He been faithful to you?"

"Yes!"

"So when you take in those negative, sabotaging voices, you're embracing a lie about who you are and rejecting the power of God to work in companionship with your faith." I also told her that those voices are not hers but the words of individuals who had spoken into her life when she was a little girl. Those detrimental messages like "You're too smart for your own good! You'll never make it! You're too tall, too short, too . . ." were still lodged in her subconscious, repeating like a keyboard stuck on "play."

Mia and I agreed that as women we can identify the enemy's voice spouting unrealistic standards of beauty and success that in reality degrade and devalue us. Mia further explained that it's difficult to navigate through a culture that defines women's identities and ultimately their perception of success when these factors are driven by brand images used to sell records and promote recording artists.

No matter how much I encouraged Mia, it was hard for her to have confidence in Abba Daddy. I realized that negative thinking was a stronghold she needed to overcome. Mia agreed to work through her fears and no longer let them take root. She developed a strategy to praise Abba Daddy when she was overwhelmed with negative thoughts.

Her lack of confidence was evident in her friendships and other relationships, which we've come to know as "codependence." Codependency is defined as "dependence on the needs of or control by another."[1] In other words, dependence on others' approval by verbal affirmations is a form of low self-esteem. I explained to Mia that fear had led her into unhealthy relationships. Relationships are unhealthy when you feel powerless to set healthy boundaries. When you feel powerless, you don't have the courage to ward off negativity, stand for your values, or separate yourself from demeaning and otherwise abusive individuals. I encouraged Mia to take an evaluation of all her close friendships and see if unconditional love was the center factor. I asked her to then be honest about the types of influences her associates were having on her, whether positive or negative. It was essential that she get to a quiet place and push the noise away so that she could clearly hear God's kind, soothing, and affirming voice. Abba Daddy saw the places and people Mia had settled for; He witnessed the most vulnerable moments of her journey and patiently waited for her to trust Him. He is the ONE who will lead her into healthy relationships.

> A healthy relationship begins with knowing the real, authentic you and believing in and practicing a new way of thinking, not only about yourself but also about Abba Daddy's ability to make you stronger, better, through life's unexpected challenges.

ଔ ଓ

To My Sisters Who Struggle with Self-Esteem: You Are Not Alone

> You have given me your shield of victory. Your right hand supports me; your help has made me great. (Psalm 18:35)

Abba Daddy knew you before you were knit in your mother's womb. When He looked into His baby room of souls, He chose *you* to be a gift to your parents. While you were in your mother's womb, He was kindly knitting you together to be *so* beautiful from the inside out. He ensured that you were protected until your time of birth. The day you were born, heaven rejoiced! Abba Daddy had also made beautiful, perfect plans for you, His baby girl! But along the way your adversary saw how beautiful, anointed, and gifted you are, and he devised a plot to try to stop Abba Daddy's divine destiny for your life. Your adversary's plan was to tell you lies, and without a defense you may have believed them. At times you are emotionally unstable, allowing negativity to rule your thoughts. You search desperately for something to identify with, so you seek it in the world. The images you see on the screens have captured your mind and act as a gatekeeper against faith, trust, and perfect love toward Abba Daddy.

Having Faith

> It is impossible to please God without faith. Anyone who
> wants to come to him must believe that God exists and that
> he rewards those who sincerely seek him. (Hebrews 11:6)

When you believe in God, you're allowing Abba Daddy to affirm you. One way He affirms you is through the holy Scriptures. Take time to discover the promises of God. There are thousands of promises to possess. Abba Daddy calls you, as His princess, "chosen," "peculiar," "unique," "a tree of righteousness bearing much fruit," "powerful," and many more wonderful affirmations to build your faith. When life situations are in opposition to your spiritual inheritance, you must hold on to God's promises as a reigning princess and take ownership of them by renewing your mind. To believe the truth (God's Word) over your circumstances and to confess those truths and live them is to take possession of *The Blessing* by faith! But the moment you believe the enemy's lies, spewing from all worldly sources, God's divine plans and purposes for your life begin to diminish. Right now you can make the decision to no longer second-guess who you really are, for the Holy Spirit of God is your identifier and security! No more making deals for yourself, for Jesus Christ is your favor! No more selling yourself, for the King of kings—Jehovah-jireh—is your provider![2] And no more striving to bless yourself, for the kingdom of Abba Daddy is your reward!

Having Trust

Perfect love casts out fear. (1 John 4:18)

When my friend, an ambitious business owner, was fearful of dumping her unfaithful boyfriend, I knew that trust in God was the missing factor. When we allow the Holy Spirit to have His way in our mind, emotions, and hearts, we are responding to true love, and this kind of love allows the power of God to forcefully cast out fear in every circumstance! This includes fear of abandonment, rejection, failure, and being alone. One of the driving forces of fear is insecurity. Insecurity breeds competition, and competition brings out the "mean girl" in women. When you trust Abba Daddy, you can joyfully celebrate others' successes while you're waiting your turn—all because you have a covenant relationship of perfect love and trust with Him.

Only Abba Daddy can give you the daddy-daughter love relationship that affirms you as His. When you believe in Him and understand that He alone is God, no matter the circumstances, you can say, "There is no other God; there never has been, and there never will be."[3] Now, that is trust!

The Power to Embrace Perfect Love

Christ will make his home in your hearts as you trust in him. Your roots will grow down into God's love and keep you strong. (Ephesians 3:17)

It takes the power of God working in your heart for you to comprehend His perfect love for you. When the ordinances of your past were against you and there was no hope for you to partake of *The Blessing*, He made the way possible through Jesus Christ, His Son. Abba Daddy made you a fellow heir of His promises, blessings, and covenant that were first made exclusive to the Hebrews. You don't have to earn or work to receive God's empowerment; He gives it freely to you because He loves you and extends His grace—unmerited favor—over you. Abba Daddy put all His blessings—*The Blessing*—in place for you before you even said yes to Him, yes to change, or yes to His call of salvation.

The Call is to a new identity, a greater purpose, a perfect love, and eternal life with Him. Answering *The Call* begins with this understanding: You have been brought near to Abba Daddy through the blood of Christ.[4] You may not know Jesus yet, you may not feel your Abba Daddy's presence yet, and you may not yet know His beautiful redemption story, but if you simply *believe* that Jesus is the way, the truth, and the life, you have accepted *The Call* and have inherited *The Blessing*.

The Blessing promises these wonderful things:

The Lord will make you the head and not the tail, and you will always be on top and never at the bottom. (Deuteronomy 28:13)

Wherever you go and whatever you do, you will be blessed. (Deuteronomy 28:6)

---

[1]*"Codependency." Merriam-Webster Online Dictionary. Webster.com. 2017. http://www.merriam-webster.com/medical/codependency (Accessed February 24, 2017.)*

[2]*Read Genesis 22:14 in the KJV or ASV.*

[3]*Read Isaiah 43:10.*

[4]*Read Ephesians 2:13.*

Chapter Six

Bound Places:

Abba Daddy Liberates

Jesus replied, "What is impossible with man is possible with God." (Luke 18:27 NIV)

"I'd run and jump into his arms, knowing I could trust my daddy to catch me. The goodnight kisses, his smile, and his caring eyes are wonderful memories I hold. At my wedding he walked me down the aisle and presented me to my groom. And he danced with me to the Luther Vandross song 'Dance with My Father.' He showed me that no mountain is too high for his love."

Lindsey shared this with a soft smile and faraway look. I knew this was not her real story but her dream. Lindsey never knew her dad.

ଓ ଓ

For some, your daddy's presence was a reality and a role model to cherish, but for Lindsey this scenario was her fantasy. Longing for a dad's love and presence stayed with her as though her dream were real. The shame of her dad's absence kept her searching for fulfillment in relationships because her mind-set was false: surely this man will love me with a daddy's love.

Searching for a dad's love in men will take you to places of bondage where women idolize relationships, sell their virtue, and perform in ways they don't want to remember. In the end, they become enslaved to their unconscious search for a daddy's love. If you have ever trafficked through such dry places, it's time to draw closer to your Abba Daddy. He is the ultimate daddy who provides liberation, and He's calling *you* into His arms of restoration.

> Behold, I am the Lord, the God of all flesh. Is anything too hard for me? (Jeremiah 32:27 ESV)

Lexy's Confession: Abba Met Me at the Crossroads

She had brown sugar caramel skin, hazel eyes, long-flowing highlighted blond hair, and a backyard (*derriere*) to complement. Lexy and I met for lunch at a five-star restaurant. She was profiling in her fabulous fitted jeans, a low-cut silk handkerchief blouse with matching red-bottom stiletto booties, an exclusive mink fur, flawless makeup, perfectly arched eyebrows, and classy matted lips. Shall I continue? Expensive twenty-four-karat gold and diamond hoop earrings, matching bangles, brightly colored gel nails, and a high-end designer bag completed her dazzling presence. When Lexy walks into a room, all heads turn. "I receive more attention than the president," she jests with a sassy shake of her head. "If you have a sexy body, then work it! I've been working it for my good," Lexy shared with a laugh. "Men have generously lavished me with many fine gifts, chauffeured me in Bentleys, and flown me in their private jets to the best exotic places and celebrity events. They're my sugar daddies, and I'm their companion."

"Where do you work, Lexy?" I interjected.

"I'm an entrepreneur. I manage several businesses. I don't want to repeat the cycle of my mother by not having enough money for rent and clothes or by being desperate for a man to live in my house, eating my food and driving my car without paying one single bill. Bye to the boys! I'm doing what I have to do to make ends meet, even if that entails being an escort to wealthy men."

Even though Lexy shared all this with haughty pride, she had a way of making even the most sanctified, church-going girl feel as if she were missing out on life. But I knew she felt a sense of sadness and shame deep inside her. So I asked, "But who is the real woman underneath all that style?" Twenty-seven-year-old Lexy couldn't identify who she was under her brand image. She confessed that even though her relationships rewarded her with many material things, her heart longed for a real relationship that was permanent and promising. I asked her how she had come to live in that unsafe lifestyle where all her confidence—her looks and admirers—was stored in one basket. When she removed her shades, I saw a woman who was tired and needed a way out. "Lexy, what's your real story? Where do you come from, and where is your father?"

Lexy's story began with her ten-year-old daughter, Grace, and with Gerald, the child's dad, who barely knew her. "My relationship with Gerald was just like my mother and father's relationship. My father was an older man who courted my mother when she was a teen, and when she became pregnant at sixteen, he left. My uncle—my mom's brother—was the surrogate father who partially raised me. He told me I could have done better than Gerald, but I had to have Gerald. Our relationship began with one date that extended two years; and, *pop*, at sixteen, there came a surprise: pregnancy. My relationship with Gerald felt like a never-ending roller coaster ride until Grace was born and our relationship ended. He wasn't responsible or available. But I don't regret having Grace. She's my gift. I just thought Gerald would have been a better father, a better provider and friend to us. Looking back, I see I could have made better choices with him and with my education and where I am now."

"That's your past," I encouraged. "What matters now is your future. Lexy, don't believe the lie."

"What lie?" she asked, perplexed.

"The lie that these types of relationships are as good as it gets. God wants to blow your cover so that He can clothe you with godly esteem! Moving forward, your heavenly Father has chosen you to make healthy choices with your life, including the best way to raise your daughter. You can be a better mother to Grace by living a lifestyle that's worth emulating, setting an example of healthy relationships that she can follow."

Lexy was quiet, and I could tell the Holy Spirit was softening her heart. "Lexy, the only love you have known is *eros* love—the sexual, erotic love our society uses to make billions from thirsty souls. I'm here to present to you the pure and true love of Abba Daddy, our heavenly Father, who has always loved you with a perfect and everlasting love. He says in His Word, 'My faithful love for you will remain. My covenant of blessing will never be broken' [Isaiah 54:10].

"Today He's calling you to experience His covenant love—a love that is a mainstay, unmovable and powerful! When Abba Daddy redeemed you, He bought you with the highest price to give you *The Blessing*. No one could ever outbid Him for you. He knew you would need security, so before you were even born He established His covenant of peace so that your enemies would stay far away and peace and protection would cover you and your daughter. His costly exchange broke the yoke of bondage for you! There's no reason to sell your priceless virtue to the god of lust and the god of your dependency on others to meet your emotional and financial needs. Your heavenly Father has set you apart and placed a crown of beauty on you, so when others see you, they will witness His awesome glory on you. He knows your makeup because He created you, and He's given you His Holy Spirit so that you'll have His power to remain loyal and faithful to Him. And let's not forget royalty! He has your tiara of real diamonds and pearls waiting for you. You're crowned as a royal daughter of God. He says in Isaiah 62:3, 'The Lord will hold you in his hand for all to see—a splendid crown in the hand of God.'

"Lexy, who has ever *loved* you like that? Who?"

After presenting that good news to Lexy, she prayed with me and then promised to keep her faith alive. Thereafter, we continued our talks, and I encouraged her to join a Christ centered church that supports her faith. Eventually we lost touch, but "I am certain that God, who began the good work within [her], will continue his work until it is finally finished on the day when Christ Jesus returns" (Philippians 1:6).

⌐ Mikki's Confession: The Princess, the Situation, and Freedom ⌐

Mikki called, spewing anger and frustration over her doctor's report. "He did it to me again, and I'm sick of this!"

"Sick of what, Mikki?" I responded.

"Another infection! And now I'm at the pharmacy again."

Even though Mikki had made a confession for Christ, she had not made Him Lord over her love life. Without purpose, direction, or the advice of an invested dad, Mikki had become involved in relationship after relationship. Her present one was with her live-in boyfriend and his two sons.

When I first met Mikki, she was twenty-three, a college student majoring in early childhood education, and in need of mentoring. She had confessed to me that she was searching for stability in her life. She was tired and needed a safe place to rest. I had asked her what type of relationship she'd had with her dad, and her response was "My dad and I had a falling out, and I haven't talked with him in three years." Then she exploded with "Why should I respect male figures when my own dad wasn't a good example?!" It was a tired and unresolved subject for her. "I really don't want to talk about him right now; it's a painful thing, you know?" I encouraged Mikki to join our Bible study group, where we keep our discussions live and real. In the following pages you'll read various excerpts on sexual integrity.

ᘓ ᘔ

Like Mikki, the common thread in women's relationship issues is linked to our dads—the first male figure of influence in our lives. Our dads were the conceptions, the beginning of relationships that led us either toward or away from the authentic love that can be found only in Abba Daddy. If your story is like Mikki's, you know what it's like to be deeply disappointed by your dad. For some, the truth is this: our dads didn't have the capacity to love us as our Abba Daddy intended. As a result, we perceived our dads' emotional absences as their rejections of us because they were not there to strengthen us emotionally, oversee our growing pains, support our many endeavors, or give us opportunities to experience daddy-daughter bonding relationships. Some of us have not been able to get over the rejections, and we're still living in a revolving cycle of unhealthy relationships.

You may still hold anger or even hatred toward your dad. Perhaps you've declared, "I will never love like my mother," or All men are dogs!" Such words are so powerful that they can sabotage *the flow of generational blessings*: healthy, godly wifehood and motherhood. I've even witnessed young women becoming involved in same-sex relationships because they're angry at their dads. Instead of seeking healing when those same-sex encounters didn't work out, they kept moving from one similar relationship to another, hoping the next one would fulfill them. You can speak either life or death about your father and men. Today let us speak life!

Mikki's Update: What about My Sexual Needs?

"How can God play a role in my love life?" Mikki asked. "I'm still dealing with some hurt, and my sexual needs are calling me."

03 80

I understand the place of wanting to do right when your flesh is pulling you to go left. My mentor said, "When you shake a soda, it will fizzle." This happens when you're living a celibate lifestyle but your flesh wants sexual gratification. Abba Daddy admonishes His princesses to keep their tops sealed and not to let anyone pop their tops or shake up those desires mentally or physically.[1]

When a woman's top has been popped, she may spend a lifetime seeking to be loved and protected. Most often the means is a promiscuous lifestyle, a place of bondage: a lifestyle of hookups, breakups, many boyfriends, pornography, and whoredom. A place where severe blows effect the soul and spirit. Whoredom falls under the word *porneía*, which means prostitution or other sexually promiscuous activity. Its secondary meaning is idolatry: placing other gods before the one true God.[2]

> Jesus replied, "I tell you the truth, unless you are born again, you cannot see the Kingdom of God." (John 3:3)

Just because you accept Jesus as Savior and Lord of your life doesn't mean your sexual desires go away. This struggle is real! After you've believed and are baptized, your spirit is new, but your soul and flesh need daily renewal; at times they will still fight to dominate your spirit-woman, the new you. You have to make a decision whom you will obey. As a princess, the first submission of obedience is your soul because sex begins in your mind. If you can't reign over your mind, how can you demonstrate self-control? How can you possess *The Blessing* or fullfill your purpose? How can you have victory—a sign of power and authority for Abba Daddy's princesses? Victory is being empowered by His Holy Spirit to say NO to your vices, NO to bad choices, and NO to desperation. But when you're desperate for liberation and sick and tired of getting futile results, then you're ready to answer *The Call* as a new woman, the new person, the new you who is born again. Therefore, work it out now. *You have the victory, in Jesus's name!*

Celibacy Is a Better Choice

> And so, dear brothers and sisters, I plead with you to give your bodies to God because of all he has done for you. Let them be a living and holy sacrifice—the kind he will find acceptable. This is truly the way to worship him. (Romans 12:1)

A princess who understands the depth, width, and height of Abba's perfect love responds with a yes to celibacy. It is her lowest reasonable act of worship to a faithful and loving God. Her denial from getting her sexual needs met is an acceptable sacrifice to Abba Daddy, and He responds to her with rewards.

According to your spiritual benefit package, *The Blessing,* you have rights to deliverance and can freely ask God to fill you with His Holy Spirit—your seal of redemption, your mark of daughterhood, and the evidence of fatherly guidance in your heart.[3] The more you yield to His Spirit in obedience, the more you will demonstrate His holiness to live a celibate and sanctified life, which is the ultimate fulfillment. Are you listening for His voice in your heart? Do you hear His call within you?

Living in holiness may mean you'll have no boyfriend until the right one finds you. This singleness may be a new normal for you. Certainly it's the safest choice against a broken heart, confusion, unwanted pregnancies, STDs, and HIV. From the beginning of time, Abba Daddy knew that if a ring was not put on the girl's finger—by the man of His divine choosing for His daughter—there would be major problems for her for a long time.

Possessing Sexual Integrity

When I was counseling Mikki, I shared, "In your season of waiting, obeying Abba is crucial to your future. Waiting on Him nurtures sexual integrity and builds strong character, like trust, faithfulness, *agape* love, and self-control. It's during times of waiting on Abba Daddy that you may feel most vulnerable and lonely, but you must remember that He is *always* by your side, Mikki. You are never truly alone. And you can also have accountability sisters for support and encouragement if you'll choose to interwine your life with a safe circle of godly, mature women."

I had become a big sister and friend to Mikki—not that I knew it all, but I knew enough to lead young women to the true Liberator, Jesus Christ.

> I have seen what they do, but I will heal them anyway! I will lead them. I will comfort those who mourn. (Isaiah 57:18)

My belief and experience is that Abba Daddy can mend the broken pieces of your soul and make you brand new and whole again. His antidote is to break the soul ties with all your lovers so He can make you complete, beautiful, and liberated to love Him first, above all others. He said, "You must love the Lord your God with all your heart, all your soul, all your strength, and all your mind" (Luke 10:27). Then you will be equipped to love the man He will present to you in His perfect way and time.

If you're ready to move from bondage to liberation and receive all the benefits of *The Blessing*, pray this prayer from a sincere longing to break the soul ties in your life:

Dear heavenly Father, I repent for being sexually involved with [name]. I renounce acts of [name it] and break all ungodly soul ties with [name them]. Abba Daddy, restore and heal my soul. I release into Your hands my heart, my will, my life, my healing, and my wholeness. In Jesus's name I pray, amen.

ᘓ ᘔ

It was a blessed day for Mikki when she prayed that prayer during our sister circle. She was elated to discover *The Blessing* Abba had created for her, including fruitful relationships. She proclaimed, "I will make it my priority to live holy as Abba Daddy requests of me."

Since that day of commitment to Christ, Mikki ended her relationship with her ex. Its been three years now, and she continues to say no when her flesh wants to say yes. She's holding it down until she says "I do." She has also made strides in her spiritual development by forgiving her dad. She began to trust Abba Daddy to have a fruitful relationship with her dad. As a result of her faithfulness to God, waiting on Him, Mikki and her dad are communicating again. The rift that was once there, God mended. What a testament to His power! She loves her dad as Abba loves her: unconditionally and without judgment.

Mikki finished her degree program and lives a purposeful life working in the education field. She serves on a community board and travels to exotic places with her sister-friends. Most importantly, Abba Daddy has healed her! No more bad health reports. Won't He do it!

---

[1]*Read Colossians 3:5.*

[2]*Read Song of Solomon 8:4.*

[3]*Read Ephesians 4:30.*

part three

A Safe Place

·⁓ Aria's Confession: She Listened and Obeyed! ·⁓

Aria and I had been talking about her relationship issues for some time. She was at a crossroads in making a decision between boyfriend A and boyfriend B. I told her to pray about it and wait for Abba Daddy to respond. Two weeks later we connected over coffee. Aria was still deliberating over the two men. I asked her, "What did Abba Daddy say?"

She looked at me with eyes of conviction and said, "You know, He has answered my prayers. I believe He said no about both men! Neither of them is the one God has for me."

I assured her, "You may not be getting what you want, but Abba Daddy knows what you need. If He's shutting the door, He's protecting you from something you can't see. If you decide to force the door by not submitting to His will for your life, then from that point on, your life will be reckless and highly risky, because you will be living outside His wings of protection."

ରେ ଅ

If you want to be empowered by Abba's fatherly guidance, wisdom, or counsel, then please make the prayer of David the psalmist your personal prayer of submission to God:

> O Lord, I give my life to you. I trust in you, my God. You are good and glad to teach the proper path to all who go astray. You will teach the ways that are right and best to those who humbly turn to You. And when I obey You, every path You guide me on is fragrant with Your loving-kindness and truth. Amen.[1]

Your Story Is About to Change

If you believe what you just prayed, your life story is about to change. Change happens when you truly humble yourself and submit to Abba Daddy's ways. Your actions say you want to be loved, covered, and fathered by the perfect Daddy. You're declaring that His wisdom is higher than your thoughts.

> Just as the heavens are higher than the earth, so are my ways higher than your ways and my thoughts higher than your thoughts. (Isaiah 55:9)

Abba Daddy Has You Covered

Abba's purpose for a dad is for him to impart wisdom to his daughter, affirm her worth, and show her unconditional love. A dad does this by protecting her, providing for her, and rewarding her. Likewise, when you fall under Abba Daddy's covering, you will get to know Him better. When you communicate with Him, when you understand Him—what He likes and doesn't like—and hear His voice responding to your prayers, you are moving from knowing Him as God to embracing Him as your Father. You are learning how to be a daughter, and allowing Him to be Abba Daddy to you.

Submission Is a Safe Place

If you've watched movies like *Women on Brewster's Place*, *Thelma and Louise*, or *The Color Purple*, the word *submit* will bring back ugly memories of men's imperfections. The good news is that Abba is not like those men, nor are there any imperfections in Him. He loves with perfect love that causes your heart to desire His ways. Choosing to submit to Abba is a mutual response to oneness with Him, to belonging to Him, and to acknowledging His fatherhood in your life. Submitting to Abba means being obedient to His Word. To embrace His authority over your life is to fully give Him your hand to lead and guide you. In this safe place you can rest and take refuge, knowing He will come through because He is faithful to you.

A dad has great influence over his daughters' perspective on relationships and men.

You can trust Abba Daddy's guidance with your relationship choices because He is the perfect father who guides you with insightful wisdom. He will confirm if your choices are safe. I talked with many young women who needed guidance with their love lives. They desired a successful career, a loving and prosperous husband, and blessed children. If these desires are not yours, that's fine too. You'll benefit in many other wonderful ways by allowing God to lead your life choices. The ultimate relationship experience can be found only with Abba Daddy, and when His daughters place Him first in their hearts, He fulfills them with many good things, above and beyond what they can imagine or hope for.

To my sisters who believe in covenant love and the benefits that come with it, I invite you to read further. Your wait is not in vain.

How wonderful is the grace of God; how wonderful is His promise to bless His own.

---

[1]*Read Psalm 25.*

Chapter Seven

The Wait

When the manifestation of *The Blessing* has been deferred, the waiting turns into emotional suffering, and a woman's commitment to a just God can be tested. It's in the waiting that hope is challenged.[1] But renewing strength is found in the Word of God—your lifeline to breathe again.

The purpose in waiting could be to bring about your heart's desire: that healthy relationship, marriage proposal, fruitful womb, successful career, prosperous business, emotional freedom, physical healing, fulfillment of your purpose, the success of your children—good things!

Abba promises He will give His daughters the desire of their hearts. In His presence there's fullness of joy when the focus is on how magnificent and big He is! Our adoration of praise moves us with passion and gives a peace of mind. Have you experienced Abba in that way? He invites you to enter into His rest while you wait.

> You will show me the way of life, granting me the joy of your presence and the pleasures of living with you forever. (Psalm 16:11)

From the Book of Esther to the Book of Ruth, Abba Daddy specifically included women's stories to strengthen His daughters in their waiting. He threaded three most common issues known to women: relational (matters of the heart), seed (matters of our children), and provisional (matters of resources). The Book of Ruth embodies all three issues. Let's take a look at her story.

Ruth's Journey

When Ruth the foreigner received the full blessing, it overtook her suddenly: "May the Lord reward you for what you have done, and may you receive a full reward from the Lord God of Israel" (Ruth 2:12 HCSB).

Like so many women, Ruth had suffered devastating losses: the unexpected death of her husband, who was the love of her life, and the deaths of his brother and father. They had been the breadwinners of the family, and their deaths left Ruth with only her grieving mother-in-law and sister-in-law. The three women were now alone, with no male protection, children, or income to cover them. In that ancient time there were no welfare or pension systems, and the family inheritance was far away in Bethlehem, the hometown of Ruth's in-laws, a place of bread and other provisions.

When Ruth's mother-in-law, Naomi, heard that her hometown was blooming with resources after a long famine, she and her daughters-in-law set out to go there. But during the journey, Naomi told the two young women to turn back and return to their own mothers' homes. Ruth didn't want to return to her childhood home, because her heart was longing for something better, something more. And what did she have to lose by uprooting her life in Moab, a place of aborted dreams? During the previous ten years she had endured harsh circumstances that took a toll on her. Now bereaved, barren, and impoverished, she realized Bethlehem and Naomi's God were the better choices.

Ruth's Covenant to Naomi

> Don't make me leave you, for I want to go wherever you go and to live wherever you live; your people shall be my people, and your God shall be my God; I want to die where you die and be buried there. May the Lord do terrible things to me if I allow anything but death to separate us. (Ruth 1:16–17 TLB)

Ruth clung to Naomi and begged her not to send her back but to allow her to continue the journey. She had heard stories of Naomi's God of miracles, Jehovah. He had brought Naomi's people out of Egypt's captivity, parted the Red Sea, and dried the ground to give His people a miraculous escape route. He had enabled them to take land from their enemies without bloodshed but by a praise shout that leveled the tall walls of Jericho! Among the unprecedented miracles that must have moved Ruth's heart was the fact that Jehovah had engrafted a gentile prostitute, Rahab, into a Hebrew family. This enabled her to partake of *The Blessing.* Ruth believed by faith that such a loving God would look favorably on her too and grant her the same access.

Ruth may have thought she needed an invitation to approach the holy and awesome Creator, so she made a covenant with Naomi, the one person Ruth knew was close to Him in heart. Ruth had witnessed Naomi to be a mature woman of faith by her acts of worship and obedience to God. Above all else, Ruth's commitment to Naomi was birthed out of her promise to honor her covenant above her longing to love again and ultimately *live* again. Each step she took on her journey was a step of faith, because her journey wasn't easy. She was determined to move with Naomi to a place called *hopeful*—a place where dreams come true.

> When you're connected with someone who knows Abba Daddy
> in a special and intimate way, you're in a position to make
> progress toward your destiny and live your purpose.

The days of travel through rough and dangerous terrain were grueling. She would be living among people she didn't know. And all the while she would be enduring her devastating grief and at times her mother-in-law's bitterness. Although Naomi was a faithful woman of God, she was also human, wrestling with human emotions, especially in times of challenge, loss, and change.

The journey was humbling for Ruth, but she kept her covenant to Naomi. Once in Bethlehem, she continued to work beneath her pay grade to make ends meet. All the while, she waited patiently for Jehovah's best: *The Blessing*.

The Wedding, Husband, and Baby

Ruth was a gleaner in the field of a wealthy man, Boaz. He was not only wealthy but a godly businessman reaping *The Blessing*. He saw Ruth and inquired of her. He pursued her as a godly gentleman should and then married her. Ruth and Boaz were the joining of two destinies as they stood beneath the chuppah, stating their holy vows of marriage. Abba's *shekinah*[2] glory rested on their union as they became one. His glorious light signified that He was at the center of their love for each other.

The result of Ruth's persistence and patience lead Abba Daddy to restore everything she had lost—and more! He rewarded her with upgrades in every area of her life: a celebratory wedding and then a beautiful baby boy, born into the lineage of King David, King Solomon, and Jesus Christ.[3] Ruth was once entangled in her family's generational cycle, but now she was engrafted as an heiress to the Hebrew promise of wealth, honor, and success.[4] From Ruth and Boaz's first encounter to *The Blessing* being fulfilled, Abba's handprints were on their lives, and His footsteps directed their story. Ruth's story was written for us in God's Word so that we— daddies' little girls—will remain hopeful in confidence that restoration and healing can happen after great losses and suffering.

Sweet Victory!

Abba Daddy empowers you to win, to dwell on the opposite side of impossibilities, and to gain victory over your enemies!

When your blessing is delayed, it doesn't mean your desires have been denied; it simply means you're waiting your turn. What's important is *how* you wait and *how* you work through your journey toward victory. So don't allow yourself to become discouraged in the waiting. Your waiting time is the opportunity to continue praying, serving, declaring, obeying, praising, and—most importantly—moving, because faith without works is dead.[5] Therefore, get up and walk with your head held high like the princess you are, because Abba Daddy's princesses never remove their crowns in the waiting.

I know many women who've weathered storms in the waiting. They stood on the promises of God until their inheritance was released into their lives. Abba Daddy knew the blows His daughters would endure, the spiritual adversaries who would try to bully them by piercing their thoughts with doubt. But they fought while wearing the armour of God, and they did not lose their ground.[6] Remember: I shared how Abba Daddy covers you through submission. He overshadows you with His Fatherly care and protection, keeping you hidden in His spiritual place where a "bozo" can't see you or find you. Abba Daddy knows your season of divine appointment, so don't think it's strange when no one is asking you out on a date.

> Never again will you be called "The Forsaken City" or
> "The Desolate Land."
> Your new name will be "The City of God's Delight"
> and "The Bride of God,"
> for the Lord delights in you and will claim you as his
> bride. (Isaiah 62:4)

In hard circumstances Ruth did not lower her expectations of Abba Daddy, nor did she question His love. She didn't take matters into her own hands, nor did she idolize relationships. Instead, she placed her faith in Naomi's extraordinary God. Ruth demonstrated that she loved Abba Daddy more than *The Blessing* He promised.

[1]*Read Proverbs 13:12.*

[2]*Schechinah. "At the heart of the idea of a Temple is the abiding presence of God. Although God is omnipresent, He has chosen to manifest His presence in certain locations and at certain times within history. This physical manifestation of God has come to be called the Shekinah." "The Abiding Presence of God" in "A Testimony of Jesus Christ: A Commentary on the Book of Revelation." Bible Study Tools. 2014. http://www.biblestudytools.com/commentaries/revelation/related-topics/the-abiding-presence-of-god.html (Accessed February 24, 2017.)*

[3]*Read Ruth 4:18.*

[4]*Read Genesis 12:2.*

[5]*Read James 2:17.*

[6]*Read Ephesians 6:10–18.*

Chapter Eight

Dispelling the Myths

When I lived in Boston, my rainbow tribe of friends extended from the colorful Caribbean to the oasis of east-coast Africa. We were celebrating each other and sharing our dream of marrying the superbly ideal man: he never cheats, and he's prosperous in every way. We saw ourselves as wealthy housewives, employing nannies, driving our children to private schools in Range Rovers, and owning six-figure businesses on the side while accessing unlimited credit to purchase Louis Vuitton (LV) bags and more. And we prided ourselves in looking glamorous in this lifestyle.

We believed we could have it all—ideal families and careers— without skipping a beat. We were hopeful and idealistic, especially when it came to the type of men we desired to marry. I remember those conversations, because they were ongoing group dialogues about our ideal Boaz. We had all agreed that the idea man would have the mature sex appeal of Denzel Washington, the swag of Laz Alonso, the body of Morris Chestnut, lips like those of LL Cool J, a smile like that of Idris Elba, the celebrity status of Matthew McConaughey, vocals like those of J. Moss, hilarious humor like that of Will Smith and Nick Cannon, and bad boy appeal like that of P. Diddy, Usher, and Nelly. We held tightly to our pinned-up collage of the perfect man.

One day as I was having my one-on-one with Abba Daddy in prayer, I mentioned the delay of my ideal man, requesting that he find me immediately. *What was taking God so long anyway?* His response was "He doesn't exist." Had Abba just said what I think He said? *But Lord, what about my movie star collage of the ideal man?* Abba dispelled the myth about what I believed the ideal man was supposed to be. That man was a fantasy of our imaginations.

Ruth Had Naomi and I Had My Girlfriends

In our sister circle of close girlfriends, we were the present-day Ruths, planning our lives without the benefit of Naomis to ground us in the realities of our dreams. Desperately looking for answers concerning our relationship problems, we turned to each other to safely compare our successes and failures. Through that sisterhood connection, I had great accountability and support. But when I reached the juncture in life where I wanted to expand my sister circle to gain more practical solutions on love, faith, and relationships, I included present-day Naomis who had attained the personal and spiritual success I desired. I learned a lot by observing them. Their examples helped prepare me to receive my heart's desires.

Before I share some nuggets of wisdom from my Naomi circle, I have a question for you. Can I be real with you? Please don't take offense but instead hear my heart of love in this truth: If you're in a cycle of breakups, burnouts, friends with benefits, and other such unhealthy relationships, it's time to change how you think.

Embracing wrong thinking with bad attitudes about relationships and love delays *The Blessing*. Abba Daddy desires that you live in *truth* by casting down imaginations and "every high thing that is exalted against the knowledge of God" (2 Corinthians 10:5 ASV).

Your willingness to embrace truth measures your level of maturity and success. I know this well, because each time I wait on the Lord and dispel myths about love, faith, and relationships, I'm positioning myself to possess *the promises of God* in my life (Leviticus 26:1–13). If you dare to learn what Ruth did to possess a faithful, wealthy husband, birth a son whose legacy included kings, gain a position as co-owner in her husband's prosperous business, and secure the book deal of a lifetime (in the Bible!), then come into my mentorship circle of Ruths and Naomis, a safe place to receive priceless nuggets of wisdom toward possessing God's total benefit package—*The Blessing*.

Dispelling the Myth that You Can Do Life on Your Own

There's something special about the way Abba chooses to bless His daughters, how honest He is with us, and how He gives us just what we need when we need it, including our unsung "sheroes" like Naomi.

Naomi embraced Ruth and demonstrated perfect love to her by being a mainstay through Ruth's relational developments. When Ruth was on the edge of receiving *The Blessing*, God used Naomi while she herself was broken. It wasn't life's circumstances that defined Naomi; it was who she was to her Abba Daddy. Out of her faith and confidence in Jehovah, Naomi was able to mentor Ruth in the way she should go.

Abba Daddy never intended for you to navigate through life alone, so He instructed today's Naomis to step in and help Generation Ruth.

> They should teach others what is good. These older women must train the younger women to love their husbands and their children. (Titus 2: 3–5)

Dispelling the Myth that Sheroes are Well Known and Famous

In the eyes of the world, sheroes are overlooked; but in Abba Daddy's eyes, they are among our key connections to attaining sustainable relationships. A shero is a mature woman of faith in Abba Daddy, a woman who dwells in His safe and secure place of peace and blessings—the very things most women seek. A shero gives us God's wisdom; she's our champion and supporter; she listens to our life challenges and gages our current mental and emotional health and maturity. She's a mentor; she's a sister; she's a *shero*.

Be discerning when choosing a shero. She's the one who will share with you the best lessons learned: how to wait for your Boaz, how to keep your marriage intact, how to raise your children, how to endure life's harshest blows, how to pray through a crisis, and how to survive by relying on the power of the Holy Spirit.[1]

Dispelling the Myth about Dating

> One day Naomi said to Ruth, "My dear, isn't it time that I try to find a husband for you and get you happily married again? The man I'm thinking of is Boaz! He has

been so kind to us and is a close relative. I happen to
know that he will be winnowing barley tonight out on
the threshing floor. Now do what I tell you—bathe and
put on some perfume and some nice clothes and go on
down to the threshing floor, but don't let him see you
until he has finished his supper." (Ruth 3:1–3)

Here is a case in which a young woman, Ruth, was in a position to
possess *The Blessing*. Naomi, her shero, understood how to close the deal,
seal the contract, and get Ruth to her destination without perforation
or penetration. Boaz saw her, inquired of her, and approached her with
giving hands. Ruth was focused, accountable, and productive; she
didn't have idle time to make the rounds on the dating circuit that could
delay her blessing. She understood her extraordinary, priceless worth.
Ruth's commitment to Naomi was from a servant heart—her giving
hand was a noble act of kindness that won Boaz's interest before he
even said hello. This is what it means to be in position to be found by a
good man. One of my Naomi friends said, "I didn't raise my daughter
to be a man's girlfriend; I raised her to be a wife."

A beautiful aspect of Ruth's story is that she followed her shero's
instructions by the leading of God's spirit. She didn't make
desperate decisions or have needy eyes, and her sexual longing
weren't driving forces to seal the deal either. She was fashionably
dressed for the eyes of only one man: Boaz. Her date attire was
beautiful and colorful, made of the finest fabrics her money could
buy; her brand image was dignity, virtue, and royalty.

Naomi taught Ruth the rules of engagement from the standpoint
of faith in Abba Daddy, who gave Ruth favor with the good man.
When we discover God's way to engage in dating, we will always
come out on top.

Dispelling the Myth that Good Men Don't Exist

When Ruth went back to her mother-in-law, Naomi asked, "What happened, my daughter?"

Ruth told Naomi everything Boaz had done for her, and she added, "He gave me these six scoops of barley and said, 'Don't go back to your mother-in-law empty-handed.'"

Then Naomi said to her, "Just be patient, my daughter, until we hear what happens. The man won't rest until he has settled things today." (Ruth 3:16–18)

Boaz was a committed, honorable man who secured and sealed the deal with Ruth in a godly manner. From yesterday to today, there are capable men willing to commit to and handle the responsibilities of being a husband. My mentor shared, "Men are naturally driven to fight wars, to be alpha males who like to win. They are capable of pursuing you, because you are worth it." It's interesting that Scripture doesn't describe Boaz's appearance, but it's very descriptive about his *character*.

Many a man proclaims his own loyalty, But who can find a trustworthy man? (Proverbs 20:6 NASB)

Take a look around you, and you may see that good men—God-honoring and God-loving men—do exist.

Dispelling the Myth that You Don't Need a Man

When Ruth and Naomi faced tragic hardships, they acknowledged God as their help and sought Him for guidance. In Abba Daddy's sovereignty, He will use whomever He chooses to divinely meet our needs. Ruth's foremost practical need was met by finding work as a gleaner, and it was in a rich man's field.

> "Where did you gather all this grain today?" Naomi asked. "Where did you work? May the LORD bless the one who helped you!"
>
> So Ruth told her mother-in-law about the man in whose field she had worked. She said, "The man I worked with today is named Boaz."
>
> "May the Lord bless him!" Naomi told her daughter-in-law. "He is showing his kindness to us as well as to your dead husband. That man is one of our closest relatives, one of our family redeemers." (Ruth 2:19–20)

The rich man was Boaz, and he would become Ruth's future husband. God had blessed Boaz with a prosperous business, and thereby Boaz was able to provide for Ruth and Naomi, get them out of foreclosure, and be a kinsman-redeemer[2] for their family lineage. Ruth was redeemed by Boaz just as we are redeemed by Christ from the yoke of bondage.

> I broke the bars of your yoke and enabled you to walk with heads held high. (Leviticus 26:13 NIV)

I've known women in relationships with men who were not stepping up to be providers and protectors. The women had to make ends meet without their men's help, causing the women to be "Big Mama in Charge." The caution in this type of life challenge is that a woman can become *too* independent, not allowing her man to be who God ordained him to be because she's taken on the errant attitude that she doesn't need her man's help in their relationship. One example is the woman who insists on paying for her engagement ring, the wedding, the honeymoon, and the place they will live. Even if you earn more than your future mate, your extreme independence deprives him of the blessing of doing his God-given part in the relationship. Respect is the greatest need of a man while love is the greatest need of a woman. When a man loves a woman with the love of Christ, it isn't necessary for the woman to take on all the responsibilities to be with him.

Give yourself permission to be honest and admit that you want a healthy, committed, good, man who is a provider and has faith in God. It's that simple.

Dispelling the Myth that You Won't Be Found by a Good Man

Women of faith know that only their heavenly Daddy can design a blessed union between a godly man and woman, so let's take our eyes off the good men and place the spotlight on ourselves as women. If you've experienced a broken heart, you know what it feels like to be guarded and even afraid to love openly. If anyone touches that tender spot of yesterday's hurt and you respond with the sharp woof of offensive words, wounding the hearer, this is a sign that you have some unsafe places that need to be healed. Before you receive the good man, work on perfecting the good woman within. Our example is the Proverbs 31 woman.

> When she speaks, her words are wise, and she gives
> instructions with kindness. (Proverbs 31:26)

Women who didn't have good examples of trustworthy men while growing up might believe all men are like the undesirable ones they've encountered. If that's your story, answer this self-evaluation: Why am I attracting these types of men? How can I reposition myself to attract good, decent relationships in every regard? When I look in the mirror, do I see myself as Abba sees me: an extraordinary, remarkable, and valuable woman who is a *good thang*? If not, it's time for change![3]

Dispelling the Myth that You Don't Need to Change

Naomi and Ruth understood change. They took a leap of faith when they left everything familiar to embrace everything new. They had the vision of a fruitful place and were moved by faith to get there. And they never looked back. Their move took not only faith but also vision and determined spirits to win. If you're in a dry place, doing the same thing year after year without prospering, it's time to change your thinking.

> Don't copy the behavior and customs of this world, but let God transform you into a new person by changing the way you think. (Romans 12:2)

It takes a humble heart to admit your need to embrace a new way of thinking. There were times my girlfriends and I overlooked good men because our thinking copied the behaviors and customs of the world. We thought we had the total package because of our professional, academic, and financial accomplishments. We were measuring our outward attractiveness by the world's standards, and it increased our appetite for the fantasy man. We were wrong.

The Proverbs 31 woman is a good starting point to measure one's attractiveness. A virtuous woman's inner beauty defines her attractiveness. She is praiseworthy and priced far above precious jewels and the world's standards of beauty. It was Ruth's character and beauty that drew Boaz's attention, because he desired a woman who possessed God's total benefit package inside and out.

> Charm is deceptive, and beauty does not last; but a woman who fears the LORD will be greatly praised. (Proverbs 31:30)

My sisters and I had to change our unrealistic and critical views of men, relationships, and ourselves to be positioned for *The Blessing*. To possess *The Blessing* requires change, and that change can begin only in you. Listen to the small, still voice of God that is encouraging you to do life His way.

Dispelling the Myth that the Wedding Is the Beginning and End to Happiness

The wedding is the event women have dreamed of since they were little girls. It's part of the celebration of a man and woman joining their lives together as one. But your wedding day was never meant to be idolized as a stopping point for your happiness.

Marriage is an ongoing ministry with your good man, a working-through and maturing process within you both. But I have witnessed women idolize their men and their relationship, putting those above Abba Daddy. They set their reasoning in the corner until they realize their men are just flesh and blood, never meant to be on Abba Daddy throne. On the other hand, I've seen women hold the wedding more important than the marriage. Both are dangerous places. There *is* a life after the wedding ceremony and honeymoon, and that life is in creating your legacy as you walk out your divine purpose. Where your purpose is, so is your gifting.

Dispelling the Myth that You Don't Have Gifts

A major concern for many women is having financial sustainability, with or without a husband. The truth is that God has already given you talents to fulfill His purpose and reap financial benefits from it.

> To one he gave five talents, to another two, to another one, to each according to his ability. (Matthew 25:15 ESV)

If you don't yet know your natural and spiritual gifts, a good place to start is exploring your inherent passions. Do you love finance? technology? business? literature? public speaking? creative arts? As you discover and begin to move in your God-given gifts, do so with the integrity of the Proverbs 31 woman. She will exercise high moral standards as she intensively and passionately works her gifts. She will be proactive with her talents to earn income to sustain her needs. She will educate herself in finances and make wise investments, including purchasing her own property if she chooses. She will not whine and complain about what she doesn't have but will work hard to gain what she desires and do so with a grateful heart. She will help solve problems instead of becoming one. She will diversify her skills and have fun putting her passions to work!

If you ask Abba, He will gift you with talents *beyond* those He gave you at birth. His Spirit is already at work in you to empower you to fulfill His divine destiny for your life, attain your dreams, and be successful in the way you should go while helping others along the way.

Dispelling the Myth that You Have Been Forgotten

You have been chosen to know me, believe in me, and understand that I alone am God. (Isaiah 43:10)

I petitioned Abba Daddy for a certain blessing, and when my desire didn't manifest, I prayed and cried and prayed and cried more while determining to stand on hope. The journey to reach sweet victory wasn't easy, but I knew Abba to be faithful. He was blessing me in many wonderful ways, yet He seemed slow in answering my specific request. Have you been there too? Have you ever thought, "Is Abba Daddy listening to me? Does He hear me? Has He forgotten me? I'm here to tell you—Abba has not forgotten you! He is working everything for your good.

But Zion said, "The Lord has forsaken me; my Lord has forgotten me."

"Can a woman forget her nursing child, that she should have no compassion on the son of her womb? Even these may forget, yet I will not forget you. Behold, I have engraved you on the palms of my hands; your walls are continually before me." (Isaiah 49:14–16 ESV)

Abba Daddy is saying the same to you, reminding you that your request is written on the palms of His hands, ever before Him. Be patient for the manisfestation of *The Blessing* as He gives you strength.

---

¹Read Ephesians 3:16.

²The relative who restores or preserves the full community rights of disadvantaged family members. The concept arises from God's covenant relationship with Israel and points to the redemption of humanity in Jesus Christ. Definition of "kinsman-redeemer" in Dictionary of Bible Themes. Edited by Martin H. Manser. 2009. https://www.biblegateway.com/resources/dictionary-of-bible-themes/7388-kinsman-redeemer. 1 May 2017.

³Read Proverbs 18:22.

Chapter Nine

It Takes a Village to Raise Our Daughters

G od restored my faith in relationships when He gifted me with a circle of strong and loving men. They were my grandfathers, stepdads, uncles, brothers, cousins, and spiritual dads. These awesome men played important roles in my personal, spiritual, and professional development. When I pause and think about my journey, I see that Abba Daddy was weaving within me all their wisdom, advice, and counsel to help me make right decisions. Even though they have daughters of their own, and no matter how their investment in me may have inconvenienced them, it amazes me how they took time to listen to me, adopt me, cover me, and protect me as a surrogate daddy. Because of their love and commitment, I am loved in a very special way.

Ava's Dream Interpretation: It's Not Always about Us

A demonic spirit was chasing my brother and me. We were running with all our might up three flights of stairs to my grandmother's

98

place. I realized this spirit was on our heels, and I couldn't outrun the demon. I stopped to fight it, but it bypassed me to pursue my brother with a vengeance. Even though I was running with my brother, the demon was no longer after me but after my brother. At that point, I realized my brother was very valuable, because through him the next generation would be seeded. To the demon he was the image of Abba Daddy, the responsibility holder, the one with the vision, the warrior who would place a band around his family, the overseer and protector, the love-giver, and the holder and cherisher of the women in his life.

My dream revealed that love, faith, and relationships are not always about the women! When I saw my brother fall, I fasely attributed it to the negative aspect of men's behavior. But instead of a nagging, a speech, or a good cussing out, my brother needed spiritual reinforcement—he needed strong warfare prayers—and I failed to practice this in many instances. The strategy of the kingdom of darkness is to divide and conquer the head (father). If the father is conquered, the whole family is in a dangerous place. *Lord, have mercy on our sons, husbands, daddies, and all the other men in our families.*

CႽ გ

Kelly's Brother

My brother was the first to introduce me to faith in Jesus. Entrusting my heart and life to Christ was the life-altering decision I so desperately needed to embrace. Thirteen wasn't too young to receive salvation, and when I did, both my brother and I were saying yes to *The Blessing*.

My brother discipled me in Christian faith and ensured that we studied the Bible and prayed together. I became his greatest supporter. I looked to him for the answers he so readily had. I remember when he sent me back up the stairs because my attire was not appropriate for my date, and I was obliged to follow his request for a modest outfit.

We were anointed as prince and princess of the King of kings to make a lasting difference in our family. We were dedicated to live out Joshua 24:15: "As for me and my family, we will serve the Lord." Abba had chosen us to carry out the generational blessings. Even though we didn't understand the choices, decisions, or consequences before us, Abba Daddy remained faithful when we were faithless. He never reneged on His covenant of love to both of us.

C3 80

Toya's Cousins

My male cousins loved me as though I were their leading female best friend. No matter where they were when I called (which was often), they answered. They were always willing to share their love stories from their male perspectives. I loved it when they gave me tidbits on love, faith, and relationships. In them I saw how men are human: they love, they hurt after a breakup, and they struggle to take care of their families. Most importantly, I saw how they desired to be men of God, whole and complete in their lives.

Toya's Uncles

My uncles weren't any different from my cousins. Knowing I was a sensitive woman, they counseled me with such care and grace; their mature wisdom anchored me. Their love was the double assurance of fatherly affirmations, and they served as the connection between me and my mother. They were the pillars of the family who each had a unique gift that opened their hearts to touch all the fatherless children in our bloodline, not just their own children. None of us felt left out of the loving care of a special uncle. They were examples of how it takes a village of strong men to raise our daughters.

 C3 80

Marie's Spiritual Dad

My spiritual dad was my pastor, who stood in the gap for me as a kinsman-redeemer. Although my pastor was the father of five beautiful daughters, Abba Daddy also gifted him to mentor me as his spiritual daughter. He was very insightful, able to discern through the scars I sometimes tried to cover with makeup and a Sunday morning smile. He knew what to say to reach the heart of the matter. For over twenty years, my pastor stood in the gap for me—that is, he prayed earnestly for me when I struggled professionally, spiritually, relationally, and in loss. He comforted me, knowing that the loss of a daddy can make a woman very vulnerable. He never skipped a beat in listening to me and advising me. What a blessing when clergy can cover the daughters of Zion with purpose and a clean heart![1]

When dads have stepped out of place or disappeared altogether, the church has the responsibility to spiritually cover their daughters. Men of God are the kinsman-redeemers of modern men: honorable men who father with the sensitivity of a spiritual counselor, ensuring they keep young women on the straight and narrow way that leads to abundant life: *The Blessing*.

෧ ෨

Sharon's Stepdad

A second dad and second chance to love again—this man was my stepdad. He was a good man, a handsome old-school gentleman. I never saw anger, rage, or violence in him. When I needed to talk, he was never too busy for me. He showed me that a man can provide for his family and cover his household with *true love* and integrity. I will never forget his acts of kindness when he placed his arm of protection around us with generosity of provision. When he paid for my undergraduate degree and said the only payback was for me to be successful, I knew my mom had married a winner.

Life is full of teachable moments, especially when love comes in unexpected ways. Under the loving care of my stepdad, my trust was renewed in little steps. He showed me how to embrace him as a dad and gave me practical advice on relationships. When my boyfriend (whom my stepdad liked) brought me home from a date in the wee hours of the morning, my stepdad said to him very sternly, "The next time you bring her home this late, you better put a ring on her finger." Now that's a critical example of why a dad (a father figure) is important!

It was a choice of faith for me to learn to trust my stepdad to take care of me. Likewise, I had the choice to learn to trust God with my vulnerable places. Countless times He showed me He had me covered in every way and circumstance. He never failed me, even when outcomes were not what I had thought or hoped they'd be. When I focused on the good, I saw my cup half full instead of half empty. Abba Daddy had promised to work out those daddy issues for my good. He is a faithful promise keeper who proved His faithfulness to me when he allowed the kinsman-redeemer to fill in the gaps of fatherhood.

I'm grateful for my stepdad's immense love and kindness and am grateful for all the awesome men who shared in raising me. They are part of my village! But their efforts to shield and protect me weren't enough to satisfy the deeper longings in me. I desired to be married to a godly husband, to bear children, to be truly healed from the inside out, to walk in perfect love, to leave a praise-worthy legacy, and to possess *The Blessing* that Abba Daddy promised through Jesus Christ. Only Abba Daddy can make provision for this measure of success and bring it to fruition. How beautiful are the promises of God, and how dependable!

ᘓ ᘔ

For all the peoples walk each in the name of its god, but we will walk in the name of the Lord our God forever and ever. (Micah 4:5 ESV)

---

[1]*Read Zechariah 9:9.*

Chapter Ten

Restored Places

Sharon's Confession: Building Healthy Relationships Began with My Dad

> Above all, keep loving one another earnestly, since love covers a multitude of sins. (1 Peter 4:8 ESV)

My dad, the man I love, is now with Jesus. The following is my love letter to him, sharing with you the journey that led me back home to the place where I embraced perfect love.

Dear Dad,

You were the first man to show me love, and in my eyes you could do nothing wrong. At six years old, I didn't have a clue that our relationship would go through changes. But now I understand that offenses will occur in relationships, disappointments will happen, and *The Blessing* will come with persecution.

Remember when I'd called, "'Daddy! Daddy! Daddy!" as you walked through Grandmother's door? All your children rushed to be the first to receive your hugs. You held the look of a proud father as we sang your praises. I'd be the first to give you a hug to show you how much I loved you. You'd say with a smile, "You're my Cookie." I was the apple of your eye. Your love I held tightly, like your warm, pure bear hugs on winter nights.

I learned that the love you had for me was different from the love you had for Mom. Even though your and Mom's love changed, your love for me remained the same. This lasting love taught me that I was a princess.

I chose sides during your relationship struggles with Mom. I'm sorry I meddled in your grown-up affairs. Now I know I should have been neutral and not taken your matters personally.

Dad, when I was sixteen we had our conflicting moments. Yes, I caused gray hairs to grow faster on you than your age. It was during those times that I wrestled with trusting you, especially when I didn't understand your decisions—like the time I went to see my BFF (and partner in crime) at her house after you'd told me no, and you grounded me for life. The thought that your daughter's virtue could be compromised not only drove you mad but also portrayed me as the good-daughter-gone-bad. You wanted to keep me safe from broken hearts and lost virginity, but I only saw you as the dad who was too strict. Daddy, I was testing your authority, exerting my will, and trying to be a grown-up too soon.

When I witnessed your inconsistencies, I rebelled. Now I wish I had stopped and listened to my heart. But because of pride, I kept on going against what you wanted for me, choosing my own way, right into my mid-twenties.

Oh, Dad, you were always available to me no matter what. I, on the other hand, was not available to you. I should have called and visited more, but instead I chose to distance myself from you. And you know what, Dad? The entire time I was running away from you, my heart was longing for you. Maybe this was why I couldn't commit to anyone long-term. My rebellion had landed me in unsafe places and brought about real-life consequences. Those choices took me farther away from a covenant relationship with a man and blinded my eyes to faith and perfect love.

It was the love of God that opened my eyes to the reality that my choices were not your fault but my own. In prayer, Abba showed me that my responses to you would influence whether I would have a healthy relationship with my husband. How I respond to, support, and respect him is all tied to you. Wow, Dad! If I had understood these truths earlier in life, things would have been different between us. How faithfully Abba redirected my path! You would be proud to know that I'm no longer living in regret but have moved forward to possess the promises of *The Blessing.*

During my reconciliation process with you, I learned your story, and I was then able to connect the dots that revealed the generational cycle in our family line. I learned that Abba Daddy had not called me to fix or correct you but to simply love you unconditionally and to honor, respect, and pray for you.

Dad, for so long I thought answers to my relationship issues were about you. I came to understand that those issues had always been about my relationship with Abba Daddy and the provisions He made two thousand years ago for my complete healing. Abba's one and only Son, Jesus Christ, took on all the sins of mankind and endured the suffering of thirty bloody lashes so that all mankind could be healed, including me. Deliverance is the provision Abba Daddy made for my wounds that were too deep for me to adequately express.

Dad, Abba hears my confessions and prayers under His protective covering as the God who heals, and I'm sharing this revelation with others so that they'll know there's a healing choice: Jesus Christ.

When you saw the change in me, Dad, you probably thought it was part of my New Year's resolution. No, it was a deep and real change! Abba Daddy was guiding me to be equipped to manage my expectations. Through the help of the Holy Spirit, I began to choose peaceful and productive thoughts, practice daily gratitude, let go of grudges, and most importantly, extend unconditional love to myself and others. As Abba Daddy has forgiven me, I'm practicing forgiving others. I've come to know that forgiveness and perfect love are signs of a princess who reigns in a high place of perfect love and authority.

Dad, as I put together the daddy pieces of my life, it created a beautiful collage, pieced together as only my heavenly Father could. That masterpiece allowed me to at last see you differently— as God sees you. This new vision of perfect love brought me closer to you. I was freed to reconnect with you beyond the surface and mend the broken places of our relationship.

Knowing that your time was coming to an end, Abba Daddy gifted us with increased time together. You and I were seated at the dining room table when I asked you, "Why were you so strict with me?"

You replied honestly, "It was the only way I knew how to love and protect you."

I knew this was your way of telling me you were sorry. Your response opened my eyes, and I didn't have to ask why anymore. I realized how blessed I am that Abba Daddy restored our relationship, so I remained silent, having decided long ago to focus on the positive things you showered on me. Your big hugs, wet kisses on my cheeks, and words of endearment were the symphony to my lyrics. You knew how to play the perfect smooth songs of security: skate nights, lunch dates at McDonald's, and our ride-or-die co-piloting, with you as my personal cabbie. I bragged about being your assistant. With pen and pad I noted each passenger we picked up. No activity was too menial for our daddy-daughter times. I'm reminiscing about how you also taught me to rollerskate, hand dance, bowl, and think outside the box. Most importantly, you taught me to forgive and to love the unlovable. It was my pleasure to place my energy into helping you with your business venture, because I wanted you to prosper under *The Blessing* too.

When Abba Daddy introduced me to my husband, He whispered to my spirit, "This is your Boaz; do you like him?" I said, "No, I love him and can't imagine my life without him!" Abba Daddy coached me through courtship with the man I would marry. Soon afterward, this man put a ring on my finger. Dad, I wish you could have been there as I walked down the aisle as a beautiful bride. You would have been so proud of my choice. He's proven to be a man of his word.

During a difficult wilderness season, I experienced unconditional love from my husband. That season was most challenging for us, but he weathered the storm with me. He looked past my faults, covered me, protected me, and provided for me just as you did. All of my husband's kindnesses are birthed from the same perfect love Abba has been showing me all along. In return, because of you, Dad, I learned how to forgive and be good to my husband. Let me tell you, Dad: this fine specimen of a man—my mate—intrigues me and provides a safe place for me to love. To honor him is not a chore because of his godly position in my life. He is worthy of my respect.

Writing this, Dad, I'm laughing as I revisit the memories of all we shared before you passed away, memories from the beginning of my life—my teenage parents holding me, their baby girl, in their arms as they celebrated my birth—to your last breath. I was there at your bedside, singing,"Lord, let Your light shine in this hospital room." My last words to you were "Daddy, I will always love you." And I will never forget your last words to me:"You're Daddy's little girl." With watering eyes, tears touching my lips, I watched as your last breath broke the chains of the enemy's lies and defined the truth of what it means to be Daddy's little girl: a blessing and a delight.

Dad, your words radiated deep in my heart, touched my soul, and embraced my spirit, giving me wings to soar higher than before. What victory! I knew you had never stopped loving me. That truth was enough to at last make me free.

Thank you, thank you, thank you, Dad, for all you did for me, including the inheritance you left to me. Every time I place the key into the lock of my home, I'm reminded of your legacy, our shared story, and how forgiveness and perfect love brought me back home to my first love, Abba Daddy.

Rest in peace,

Your grateful daughter

C３ ８０

**To contact author
or to place an order:**

Sharon Patterson

P.O. Box 1613

Clinton, MD 20735

The Nehemiah Projects

Smpcookie